B04704

Ph...
Development

This book is to be returned on or before the last date stamped below.

B04704

618.92
COO

LIBREX

ballymoney

nrc
northern regional college
Learning Resource Centre

Other titles in the Supporting Development in the Early Years Foundation Stage series

Also available from Continuum

Physical Development

Linda Cooper and
Jonathan Doherty

Supporting Development in
the Early Years Foundation Stage

continuum

Continuum International Publishing Group

The Tower Building	80 Maiden Lane
11 York Road	Suite 704
London SE1 7NX	New York, NY 10038

www.continuumbooks.com

© Linda Cooper and Jonathan Doherty 2010

Pictures 1.1, 1.2, 1.4, 2.3, 3.1 and 3.5 used by kind permission of Paul Hopkins - MMI educational consultancy services - http://www.mmiweb.org.uk
Pictures 1.3 used by kind permission of Emma Jordan E-Services *www. emmajordan-eservices.co.uk*
Pictures 1.5, 2.4, taken by L Nahmad-Williams and used by kind permission by Crowle Primary School

All rights reserved. No part of this publication may be reproduced or transmitted in any form or by any means, electronic or mechanical, including photocopying, recording, or any information storage or retrieval system, without prior permission in writing from the publishers.

Linda Cooper and Jonathan Doherty have asserted their right under the Copyright, Designs and Patents Act, 1988, to be identified as Author of this work.

British Library Cataloguing-in-Publication Data
A catalogue record for this book is available from the British Library.

ISBN: 978-1-4411-2400-5 (hardcover)
        978-1-4411-9244-8 (paperback)

Library of Congress Cataloging-in-Publication Data
Cooper, Linda.
  Physical development / Linda Cooper and Jonathan Doherty.
      p. cm. – (Supporting development in the early years foundation stage)
  Includes bibliographical references and index.
  ISBN: 978-1-4411-2400-5 (hardback)
  ISBN: 978-1-4411-9244-8 (pbk.)
  1. Children–Growth. 2. Motor ability in children. 3. Child development.
  I. Doherty, Jonathan, 1961– II. Title. III. Series.

RJ131.C63 2010
618.92–dc22

                                                         2010002898

Typeset by Newgen Imaging Systems Pvt Ltd, Chennai, India
Printed and bound in Great Britain by the MPG Books Group

Contents

Author Details

The two authors of this book have expertise in early years physical development in a variety of contexts.

Linda Cooper

Linda is a Senior Lecturer in Early Childhood Studies at Portsmouth University, UK. Prior to this she was a primary school teacher in West Sussex and a lecturer in higher education working with Initial Teacher Training students. Linda's specialisms are dance and ICT. Pursuing her interest as an ICT coordinator, Linda spent time gaining her MSc in Information Systems where she was involved in studying and designing educational applications. Linda also has a longstanding interest in dance and has participated in many types of movement ranging from jazz and contemporary dance to the Alexander Technique – she gained her first degree in dance in 1993. Her interest in movement has been continued throughout her teaching career. She has recently taught physical development in early childhood and PE to student teachers at Bishop Grosseteste University College Lincoln, UK.

Jonathan Doherty

Jonathan has worked in education for over 22 years. He was a Primary teacher for 9 years before moving to Leeds Metropolitan University, UK. He later became Principal Lecturer and Head of Early Childhood Education and instigated the first degree courses for early years teachers. His research is focused on child development, health and physical activity and narrowing the gap in outcomes for children. Jonathan has worked as a national consultant and served on various education committees. He has presented to national and international audiences and alongside other publications, this is Jonathan's fifth book. He now works as an Education Adviser.

Series Editors' Preface

Introduction to the series

Before the 10 year strategy (DfES, 2004) and the Childcare Act of 2006, provision for children under 5 years of age was encompassed in a variety of guidance, support and legislation; *Curriculum Guidance for the Foundation Stage* (QCA, 2000), the *Birth to Three Matters* framework (Surestart, 2003), and the *National Standards for Under 8s Daycare and Childminding* (DfES, 2003). This was confusing for many professionals working with young children. The introduction of Early Years Foundation Stage (DCSF, 2008), brought together the main features of each and has provided a structure for the provision of care and education for children from birth to 5 years of age. More importantly it recognized the good practice that existed in each sector of provision and gives a framework or support for further development.

Learning in the Early Years Foundation Stage

The four themes that embody the principles of the Early Years Foundation Stage (EYFS), (DCSF, 2008) succinctly embody the important features of early years provision.

A Unique Child, identifies the importance of child centred provision, recognizing the rapid development in young children and that each child is capable of significant achievements during these years. It is important not to underestimate young children, who may be capable of action, thinking beyond our expectations. It is easy to think that children are too young or not experienced enough to engage in some ideas or activities, but we need to be open-minded as children are very good at exceeding our expectations. Some children may have particular talents, whilst others may be 'all-rounders'. Some children may have particular needs or disabilities. Each child is unique and it is our challenge to ensure that we meet their particular needs, supporting them and challenging them in their development.

Positive Relationships are essential whilst we support and challenge children so that they move from dependence to independence, familiarity to unfamiliarity, learning how to be secure and confident individuals who begin to understand themselves and others. Positive relationships are key to all areas of children's development. Emotional development requires children to have attachments and positive relationships, initially with close family members, but increasingly with secondary carers, peers and other adults. The link between emotional and social development is very strong and positive relationships will also help children to become independent and develop new relationships and begin to see their position and role in society. Positive relationships also support language development, understandings about the world, a range of skills and indeed play a part in all development.

The context in which children develop play a vital part in supporting them in all areas of development. These contexts need to be **Enabling Environments**, or environments that are secure and make children feel confident, that stimulate and motivate children and which support and extend their development and learning. The environment is made up of the physical and the atmospheric. Both need to be warm and secure, so that children feel safe and comfortable and both need to be motivating to encourage children to explore and learn. The environmental atmosphere is also created by the social interactions of all concerned, providing the security that enables a child to move away from the familiar and explore the unfamiliar in a secure and safe way. Indoor environments should provide opportunities for social interaction, language development and creative activities. Outdoor environments may encourage children to develop physically and an interest in the world around them and with opportunities to explore the familiar and unfamiliar world.

Learning and Development indicates the importance of individual children's unique development and learning. As every child is unique, so they have different learning and development needs and will develop in different ways and at different rates. It is important not to assume that all children develop at the same rate. We know that some children begin to walk or talk at a very early age, whilst others take longer, but this does not indicate what they are capable of achieving later in life. Provision for all children needs to be differentiated. In the early years, this is best done by open-ended activities and differentiated interaction and support. Open-ended activities allow children to use and develop from previous experiences and to differentiate for themselves. Support through modelling, questioning and direction can come from experienced peers and adults and will enable the individual child to develop at a rate appropriate for them.

Working within the Early Years Foundation Stage is not without it challenges. Whilst the principles recognize the individual nature of children and their needs, providing this is a different matter. The Early Years Foundation Stage encompasses children in two traditionally distinct phases of development; from birth to 3 years of age and from 3 to 5 years of age. It involves the integration of three overlapping, but traditionally distinct areas of care; social, health and education. Children will have different needs at different ages and in different areas and stages within the EYFS and the challenge is for professionals to meet these diverse needs. It maybe that the norm for children at each age and stage is quite wide and that as many children fall outside of the norm as within it. Care is needed by professionals to ensure that they do not assume that each child is 'normal'.

In order to effectively support children's development in the Early Years Foundation Stage professionals need to have an understanding of child development and share knowledge and understanding in their area of expertise with others whose expertise may lie elsewhere. Professionals from different areas of children's care and provision should work together and learn from each other. Social care, health, educational professionals can all learn from an integrated approach and provide more effective provision as a result. Even within one discipline, professionals can support each other to provide more effective support. Teachers, teaching assistants, special needs coordinators and speech therapists who work in an integrated way can provide better support for individuals. Paediatricians, paediatric nurses, physiotherapist, opticians etc., can support the health care and physical development of children in a holistic way. Early years professionals, behaviour therapists and child psychologists can support the social and emotional development of children. This notion of partnership or teamwork is an important part of integrated working, so that the different types of professionals who work with young children value and respect each other, share knowledge and understanding and always consider the reason for integration; the individual child, who should be at the heart of all we do. Good integrated working does not value one aspect of development above all others or one age of children more than another. It involves different professionals, from early career to those in leadership roles, balancing the different areas of development (health, social, emotional and educational) and ages, ensuring that the key principles of good early years practice are maintained and developed through appropriate interpretation and implementation of the Early Years Foundation Stage.

Another challenge in the Early Years Foundation Stage is to consider the child's holistic progression from birth, through the EYFS to Key Stage 1 and beyond. Working with children in the Early Years Foundation Stage is like being asked to write the next chapter of a book; in order to do this effectively, you need to read the earlier chapters of the book, get to know the main characters and the peripheral characters, understand the plot and where the story is going. However, all the time you are writing you need to be aware that you will not complete the book and that someone else will write the next chapter. If professionals know about individual children, their families, home lives, health and social needs, they will understand problems, issues, developmental needs and be better placed to support the child. If they know where are child will go next, about the differences between the provision in the EYFS and KS1 and even KS2 (remembering the international definition of early childhood is birth to 8 years of age), they can help the child to overcome the difficulties of transition. Transitions occur in all areas of life and at all ages. When we start new jobs, move house, get married, meet new people, go to university, the transition takes some adjustment and involves considerable social and emotional turmoil, even when things go smoothly. As adults we enter these transitions with some knowledge and with a degree of choice, but young children are not as knowledgeable about the transitions that they experience and have less choice in the decisions made about transitions. Babies will not understand that their mother will return soon, small children will not understand that the friends that they made at playgroup are not attending the same nursery or that the routines they have been used to at home and at playgroup have all changed now that they have gone to nursery or started in the foundation unit at school. Professionals working with children, as they move though the many transitions they experience in the first 5 years, need to smooth the pathway for children to ensure that they have smooth and not difficult transitions.

An example of holistic thematic play

Whilst sitting outside a café by the sea in the north of England, the following play was observed. It involved four children representing the whole of early years from about 2 years of age to about 8 years of age; one was about 2 years of age, another about 3 years of age, one about 5 years of age and the fourth about 7 or 8 years of age. The two older children climbed on top of a large wooden seal sculpture and started to imagine that they were riding on top of a swimming seal in the sea. They were soon joined by the 3-year-old child who sat at the foot of the sculpture. 'Don't sit there' said the eldest, 'You are in the sea, you will drown. Climb on the tail, out of the sea'. The two older children helped the 3 year old to climb onto the tail and she and the 5 year old started to slide down the tail and climb up again. Then the children began to imagine that the cars parked nearby were 'whales' and the dogs out with their owners were 'sharks' and as they slid down the tail they squealed that they should 'mind the sharks, they will eat you'. The 5 year old asked what the people sitting outside the café were and the 8 year old said 'I think they can be fishes swimming in the sea'. 'What about the chairs and tables?' asked the 3 year old, to which the older children replied that, 'they can be fishes too'.

At this point, the 2 year old came up to the children and tried to climb up the seal. The three children welcomed her, helped her climb up onto the tail and join them and asked her what her name was. They continued to play and then the mother of the eldest child came to see if the 2 year old was ok and not being squashed in the sliding down the tail. The children did not welcome the interference of an adult and asked her to go away, because 'we are playing, we are playing'. The mother helped the 2 year old to climb down off the seal and the child started to 'swim' on the floor back towards the seal and the other children. The mother said, 'Oh you are getting dirty, get up', but the child kept on 'swimming'. 'Are you being a dog' said the mother 'don't crawl', but the child shook her head and carried on 'swimming' towards the seal, avoiding the fish and sharks!

In this play episode, the children were engaged in holistic play involving aspects of

- Personal, Social and Emotional Development (cooperation);
- Language, Literacy and Communication (communicating with each other and with adults);
- Knowledge and Understanding of the World (applying ideas about animals that live in the sea);
- Creative Development (imaginative play, involving both ludic or fantasy play and epistemic play, or play involving their knowledge).

The adult intervention was, in this case, unhelpful and did not aid the play and illustrates the importance of adults standing back and watching before they interact or intervene.

Supporting development in the Early Years Foundation Stage

This book series consists of six books, one focusing on each of the key areas of the Early Years Foundation Stage and with each book having a chapter for each of the strands that make up that key area of learning. The chapter authors have between them a wealth of expertise in early years provision, as practitioners, educators, policy-makers and authors and are thus well placed to give a comprehensive overview of the sector.

The series aims to look at each of the key areas of the EYFS and support professionals in meeting challenges of implementation and effectively supporting children in their early development. The aim is to do this by helping readers, whether they are trainee, early career or lead professionals:

- to develop deeper understanding of the Early Years Foundation Stage,
- to develop pedagogical skills and professional reflectiveness,
- to develop their personal and professional practice.

Although the series uses the sub-divisions of the key areas of learning and strands within each key area, the authors strongly believe that all areas of learning and development are equally important and inter-connected and that development and learning for children in the early years and beyond is more effective when it is holistic and cross curricular. Throughout the series, links are made between one key area and another and in the introduction to each book specific cross curricular themes and issues are explored. We recognize that language development is a key element in social and emotional development, as well as development in mathematics and knowledge and understanding of the world. We also recognize that the development of attitudes such as curiosity and social skills are key to development in all areas, recognizing the part that motivation and social construction play in learning. In addition, the books use the concept of creativity in its widest sense in all key areas of development and learning and promote play as a key way in which children learn.

Although we believe it is essential that children's learning be viewed holistically, there is also a need for professionals to have a good knowledge of each area of learning and a clear understanding of the development of concepts within each area. It is hoped that each book will provide the professional with appropriate knowledge about the learning area which will then support teaching and learning. For example, if professionals have an understanding of children's developing understanding of cardinal numbers, ordinal numbers, subitizing and numerosity in problem solving, reasoning and numeracy then they will be better equipped to support children's learning with developmentally appropriate activities. Although many professionals have a good understanding of high quality early years practice, their knowledge of specific areas of learning may vary. We all have areas of the curriculum that we particularly enjoy or feel confident in and equally there are areas where we feel we need more support and guidance. This is why each book has been written by specialists in each area of learning, to provide the reader with appropriate knowledge about the subject area itself and suggestions for activities that will support and promote children's learning.

Within each chapter, there is an introduction to the key area, with consideration of the development of children in that key area from birth to 3 years of age; 3 to 5 years of age; into Key Stage 1 (5 to 7 years of age). In this way we consider the holistic development of children, the impact of that development on the key area and the transition from one stage of learning to another in a progressive and 'bottom-up' way. Chapters also contain research evidence and discussions of and reflections on the implications of that research on practice and provision. Boxed features in each chapter contain practical examples of good practice in the key area, together with discussions and reflective tasks for early career professionals and early years leaders/managers, which are designed to help professionals at different stages in their career to continue to develop their professional expertise.

Jane Johnston and Lindy Nahmad-Williams

Books in the series

Broadhead, P., Johnston, J., Tobbell, C. & Woolley, R. (2010) *Personal, Social and Emotional Development.* London: Continuum

Callander, N. & Nahmad-Williams, L. (2010) *Communication, Language and Literacy.* London: Continuum

Beckley, P., Compton, A., Johnston, J. & Marland, H. (2010) *Problem Solving, Reasoning and Numeracy.* London: Continuum

Cooper, L., Johnston, J., Rotchell, E. & Woolley, R. (2010) *Knowledge and Understanding of the World.* London: Continuum

Cooper, L. & Doherty, J., (2010) *Physical Development*. London: Continuum

Compton, A., Johnston, J., Nahmad-Williams, L. & Taylor, K. (2010) *Creative Development*. London: Continuum

References

DCSF (2008) *The Early Years Foundation Stage; Setting the Standard for Learning, Development and Care for Children from Birth to Five; Practice Guidance*. London: DCSF

DfES (2003) *National Standards for Under 8s Daycare and Childminding*. London: DfES

DfES (2004) *Choice for Parents, the Best Start for Children: A Ten Year Strategy for Children*. London: DfES

QCA (2000) *Curriculum Guidance for the Foundation Stage*. London: DFEE

Surestart, (2003) *Birth to Three Matters*. London: DfES

Introduction to Physical Development

Physical development

Physical development covers a wide range of fine and gross motor skills and understandings about physical development, as well as linking with aspects of health and physical development covered in *Self Care* (see Broadhead et al., 2010). Concerns about physical development (e.g. Palmer, 2006: 60) focus around the *'loss of opportunities for outdoor, loosely supervised play'*, which is adversely affecting both social and physical development. Parents and carers are so worried about child safety and this, combined with the increase in working parents and pressures on children, means that children have fewer opportunities for walking in the park, playing in the playground, going swimming etc. Indeed parental responsibility for physical development appears to have been passed to formal settings and carers. For example, one parent, on being surveyed about a school's homework statement, identified that they did not have time to take their child to a park and it was the school's responsibility to do this.

The link between physical and mental health has been known for many years (e.g. McMillan, 1911; Gallahue and Ozmun, 2006), but physical development is important in all areas of development. Fine motor skills are needed in mark-making in *Communication, Language and Literacy* (see Callander and Nahmad-Williams, 2010) and in handling mathematical apparatus and writing numbers in *Problem-Solving, Reasoning and Numeracy* (see Beckley et al., 2010). In *Knowledge and Understanding of the World* (see Cooper et al., 2010) children need fine motor skills to handle technical equipment, make and measure. In *Creative Development* (Compton et al., 2010) children need gross and fine motor skills to engage in creative activities, such as dance, role-play and art. In *Personal, Social and Emotional Development* (see Broadhead et al., 2010) the link between physical development and *self care* has already been mentioned, but Broadhead (2004) has also identified the link between rough and tumble play and social development, by helping children to negotiate boundaries.

Holistic physical development

Physical development begins in the womb and initially children's reflexes dominate and their movements are uncoordinated. They acquire gross motor skills in a sequential manner by meeting 'milestones', which we use to ascertain how their development meets the 'norm'. However, we must remember that the acquisition of skills will not be the same for every child, as each child is individual and the 'norm' covers a wide variation of development. Major milestones like crawling and walking are followed by periods of consolidation when children practice physical activities and refine their motor skills, becoming more coordinated, balanced and agile, so that they can walk with confidence and even run. They learn to balance on one leg, or on increasingly narrower objects. They learn to use their eye-hand coordination to hit a ball with a bat.

Physical development is affected by both genetics and environmental factors. Body type, inherited physical traits are balanced by opportunities, encouragement, support and resources available. Important in physical development are physiological needs, which Maslow (1968) identified as the foundation of his hierarchy of needs. If these physiological needs are not met, then children will not be able to move up the hierarchy and realize their potential in life. Physiological needs are needed to enable children to concern themselves with safety needs and these in turn need to be met to achieve emotional needs and esteem needs and finally the pinnacle of the hierarchy, self actualisation. So problems in physical development can affect all other areas of development.

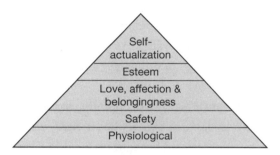

Figure 0.1 Maslow's (1968) Hierarchy of Needs

The importance of physical development, health and learning were recognized by Rachel and Margaret McMillan. They recognized that a healthy body led to a healthy mind (McMillan, 1911), emphasizing the part good nutrition plays on both physical and cognitive development in both the early years and throughout an individual's whole life (McMillan, 1930). Today, problems of poor nutrition are still important, with young children just as likely to suffer physically, emotionally, socially and educationally, through obesity and eating the wrong balance of food as from lack of food and malnutrition.

Examples of holistic cross-curricular physical development

In this book, as in the other books in this series, we recognize that physical development occurs in holistic cross-curricular ways, through play and exploration.

The building site

In a nursery school, the outside play area was set up as a building site. Large foam building blocks, a tunnel, a wooden balance bench and a climbing frame formed part of the 'building site'. Hard hats, dungarees and Wellington boots were set out so children could be in role as builders and toy tool sets were used to enhance imaginative role-play. Clipboards with paper and pencils attached by string were prepared so that the children could design structures.

One morning in the nursery, two groups of children were involved in parallel play; one using the 'building site' for being 'Bob the Builder' and the other for being 'Rapunzel'. Both involved a range of physical skills.

Diara arrived early and sat in the building site and reading a book. He was joined by Dan who asked if he wanted to play 'Bob the Builder' (see BBC, 2009). They dressed themselves in dungarees and put on belts and hard hats and Wellington boots.

'We have to mend this door', said Diara, pointing to the wooden door on the play house in the outside play area. Dan replied *'It needs drilling, let's get a drill'*. Diara went to the toy tool box and brought back a drill. Dan said, *'I want one too'* and Diara went and got another one for Dan and they began to mend the door. After a little while, the two boys were joined by Joel and Katy who decided that the door needed to be painted, so they got a bucket, which they filled with water and two large paint brushes and they began methodical to paint the door with the water. *'You've missed a bit'* said Dan, pointing to a dry bit of the door and both Joel and Katy painted over the 'missed bit'. *'Are there other bits to mend?'* said Diara and all fours children looked around. *'Yes, I think we need to mend this bit'* and they got the drills and a screwdriver and a paint brush and moved over to the fence and gate to do some mending.

Meanwhile Sophie put on a hard hat and high heeled shoes and picked up a clip board. She made some marks on it and walked around the 'building site', making marks on her clipboard. *'We need a big tower'* she said, and Peta asked if they could build a tower for Rapunzel to go in. *'It will have to be big for Rapunzel'*, said Sophie and they started to build a tall structure with foam bricks, but it kept falling down. The professional came and suggested that they built the bottom of the tower wide and the tip smaller and so Sophie and Peta began to build a more balanced structure. *'Let's make it four high'*, said Sophie. *'No five, five'*, said Peta. When they had built the tower, the girls decided to dress up and went to the dressing up box inside the class. Sophie decided she wanted to be Rapunzel, but so did Peta so the professional suggested that they were both Rapunzel; Rapunzel 1 and Rapunzel 2. *'Can we play too?'* said Sarbjit and Anton. *'We can be knights rescuing her'* said Anton and he and Sarbjit found put on dungarees and hard hats to pretend to be 'knights'.

Sophie and Peta went to their tower and waited while the other two children 'galloped' around the play area, climbed up the climbing frame, which they pretended to be a 'mountain' and walked across the bench which was a 'drawbridge' and crawled through the tunnel which was the entrance to the tower. *'Rapunzel, Rapunzel, let down your hair'*, said Sarbjit. Once the girls had come down the tower, they all crawled through the tunnel and started to go across the bench, but Peta could not balance, so Anton held her hand and helped her. Sophie asked the professional if they could use the camera to take a picture of Anton helping Peta and then she told the two children to wait while she got it to take a picture for the assessment profile. *'Take some more'*, said the professional and so Sophie took some pictures of the others and then Anton took one of Sophie and Peta being Rapunzel by the tower waiting for rescue.

In this way the children were physical by engaging in fine motor skills (drawing, writing, dressing) and gross motor skills (crawling, climbing, balancing, building). In addition to the physical development, the children were developing other key areas of the Early Years Foundation Stage (DCSF, 2008).

- Personal, social and emotional development; by taking and negotiating on roles (see Broadhead et al., 2010)
- Communication, Language and Literacy; by communicating with each other and mark-making (see Callander and Nahmad-Williams, 2010)
- Problem-solving, reasoning and numeracy, by counting the foam blocks and calculating how high they could build the structures (see Compton et al., 2010)
- Knowledge and understanding of the world by using and handing tools, ICT and testing the strength of structures (see Cooper et al., 2010)
- Creative development; by using their imagination in their role-play, building on their previous knowledge and stories and using them in imaginative contexts (see Compton et al., 2010).

Structure of this book

There are three areas involved in the key area of *Physical Development* and these are represented in the three chapters of this book. In Chapter 1, Linda Cooper looks at children's development in *Movement and Space* throughout the Early Years Foundation Stage. Jonathan Doherty looks children's *Health and Bodily Awareness* in Chapter 2 and their use of resources in Chapter 3, *Using Equipment and Materials*.

The case studies and reflective tasks will also help professionals to reflect on their own practice, consider the theories and research underpinning effective practice and enable them to identify how they can (and why they should) develop their practice. These case studies are designed at two levels; the early career professional and the early years leader. The early years professional may be a student/trainee who is developing their expertise in working with young children and, for them, the reflective tasks encourage them to look at the case studies and engage in some critical thinking on issues that are pertinent for early years education. They will also be able to use the chapters to develop their understanding of issues and skills in physical development and try out some of the ideas to develop their skills supporting children in this important area of development. The reflective tasks for early career professionals are also relevant to professionals who are in the early part of their career and to help them in their day to day interactions with children but also to help them to engaged in the national debates about good practice and educational theories. The second level of reflective tasks are geared towards the early years leader, who has a strategic role to develop the practice of those who work with them but also the children in the early years setting. They would be interested on the impact on both the adult professional development but raising standards in physical development in young children in their setting. The reflective tasks may well be ones that can be addressed as part of a staff meeting or staff development session and can follow the practical tasks so that professionals at all levels can share ideas and experiences, identify factors affecting their support for children, both positive factors and challenges to overcome. In this way professionals can discuss their own and other's practice, share successes, support each other and come to realize that there is not one model of good practice, one recipe, that if we all follow will automatically lead to success in children's development and help the setting achieve outstanding recognition in inspections.

Summary

The main issues in this book are as follows:

- Physical development involves understandings about health and physical attributes, as well as fine and gross motor skills.

- Young children need to be active and given opportunities to practice and refine their physical skills.
- The refinement of physical skills helps children in other areas of development, such as handling equipment in *Knowledge and Understanding of the World* or *Problem-Solving, Reasoning and Numeracy* and mark-making in *Communication, Language and Literacy.*
- Physical development is an important component in healthy living and the EYFS is a good opportunity to begin this.
- Physical development can be enhanced using a range of resources and equipment.
- Children need to be encouraged and supported to enable them to move to the next stage of physical development.

We hope that professionals reading this book both enjoy and find the content useful in their professional lives.

References

BBC. (2009) Bob the Builder website http://www.bbc.co.uk/cbeebies/bobthebuilder/

Beckley, P., Compton, A., Johnston, J. and Marland, H. (2010) *Problem Solving, Reasoning and Numeracy.* London: Continuum

Broadhead, P. (2004) *Early Years Play and Learning. Developing Social Skills and Cooperation.* Abingdon, Oxon: RoutledgeFalmer

Broadhead, P., Johnston, J., Tobbell, C. and Woolley, R. (2010) *Personal, Social and Emotional Development.* London: Continuum

Callander, N. and Nahmad-Williams, L. (2010) *Communication. Language and Literacy.* London: Continuum

Compton, A., Johnston, J., Nahmad-Williams, L. and Taylor, K. (2010) *Creative Development.* London: Continuum

DCSF. (2008) *The Early Years Foundation Stage; Setting the Standard for Learning, Development and Care for Children from Birth to Five; Practice Guidance.* London: DCSF

DfES. (2004) *Choice for Parents, the Best Start for Children: A Ten Year Strategy for Children.* London: DfES

Gallahue, D. and Ozmun, J. (2006) *Understanding Motor Development. Infants, Children, Adolescents, Adults,* 6th edition. New York. McGraw-Hill

Maslow, A. H. (1968) *Towards a Psychology of Being.* New York: D. Van Nostrand Co

McMillan, M. (1911) *The Child and the State.* Manchester: National Labour Press

McMillan, M. (1930) *The Nursery School.* London: Dent

8 Physical Development

Palmer, S. (2006) *Toxic Childhood. How the Modern World is Damaging our Children and What we can do about it.* London: Orion

QCA. (2000) *Curriculum Guidance for the Foundation Stage.* London: DFEE

Surestart. (2003) *Birth to Three Matters. A Framework to Support Children in their Earliest Years* London: DfES

Movement and Space

Chapter Outline

Introduction

This chapter seeks to address the very central importance of movement in the overall holistic development of a child. Movement and the successful acquisition of gross, locomotor and fine motor skills have overarching implications for all areas of learning. Children need to be given plenty of time and opportunity to develop and refine movement. This chapter explores the different stages of development of movement skills. It also discusses how to create effective learning opportunities that encourage physical development from birth through to the transition into Key Stage 1.

Movement and space from birth to 3 years of age

Learning to move is key for very young children. When a child can move he/she can expand their horizons, learn about the world and make choices as to how they experience their environment. Learning to move is one the most noticeable developments in a young child's life and often much anticipated by attentive parents and the extended family. A child's first steps are the cause of much comment and excitement; occasionally it can be a source of pride that 'Charlie' was the first to move out of all of his friends. This can lead to a sense of achievement for some and perhaps anxiety in other parents as to when their child will make progress in movement activity. A child's first steps accompany a sense of change, growth and development; the child is leaving the realms of early infancy and becoming a toddler who can more quickly assert it's independence and detach itself from his/her parents. At this early stage of life concerns and celebrations about movement acquisition make-up the detail of numerous conversations between parents and child minders/nursery staff. Practitioners working with children at this age need to know about physical development. This knowledge will aid in the creation of effective environments in which to promote healthy physical development.

Although a newborn child appears helpless he/she is equipped with a number of involuntary reflexes which are responsible for early movement. These reflexes are triggered in response to stimuli and provoke involuntary reactions in the child. Reflexes are present to help children survive and to aid them through their first weeks of life. For example, babies are born with the inbuilt ability to 'root' and 'suck' which allows them to gain nutrition from their mothers (Cooper, 2008) Primitive reflexes disappear in the first months of life and are replaced by observable motor skills.

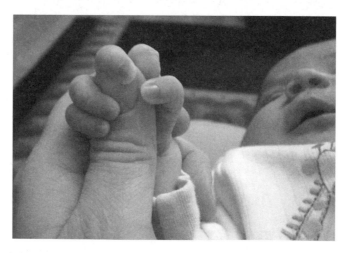

Photograph 1.1 Reflexes in a Newborn baby (© P. Hopkins)

Goddard Blythe (2005) notes the connection between reflex development and early learning that reveals the importance of physical development even from the very start of life. She suggests that an incomplete transition from primitive reflexes to early motor development can result in problems in balance and coordination. For instance, retained rooting and sucking reflexes can interfere with the development of clear speech patterns and the coordination of the mouth muscles. Her educational programme focusing on movement to correct immature reflexes appears to have great beneficial consequences for the academic progress of the children involved.

Vital changes in the wiring of the brain in the region of the cerebral cortex help children move from involuntary reflexes to voluntary movement. The importance of movement in initiating developments in the brain cannot be underestimated. David et al. (2003: 124) state that 'providing movement experience is essential to brain development and brain development is essential in taking advantage of the experience'. When a baby achieves a certain physical milestone this experience expands the child's interaction with the world and this in turn stimulates increased synaptual development in the brain. These authors go on to argue that by being given plenty of opportunities to move babies 'map' their spatial environment that allows them to make mental images of a place and this subsequently makes them more secure and confident.

The sequence in which children learn to move follows a predetermined pathway.

Cephalocaudal growth pattern is the sequence in which growth occurs. The fastest growth happens at the top of the body which gradually works its way down from the neck to the shoulder and then to the trunk and lower body. When babies are born the head makes up ¼ of a child's overall body weight (Santrock, 2007: 139).

Proximodistal development is the growth pattern that starts at the centre of the body and moves towards the extremities (Santrock, 2007: 139).

As children develop they will move through similar milestones gaining more and more control over their body. *Developmental milestones* are a set of functional skills or age-specific tasks that most children can do at a certain age range (Kyla Boyce, 2009). It is useful to know which movement milestones are associated with which age group so as to be able to ascertain whether a child's movement development is on track. It is also beneficial to know that checklists that record milestones only give an approximate guide and that some children may pass through a milestone at a different speed than others. There is not necessarily anything medically wrong with a child, for instance, who is slower to walk than another, each individual's speed of development is unique. What a practitioner must be aware of is when a delayed growth pattern becomes sustained and noticeable and might start to negatively influence overall global development.

Practical task

Look at the developmental milestones listed below – these are all milestones a child should pass through before the age of 20 months. Can you put them into a chronological order? Can you apply an approximate age range when you would think a child should be demonstrating the movement?

- Turns head or eyes towards diffuse light or interesting objects
- Crawls, bottom shuffles or rolls continuously to move around
- Demonstrates strong reflex movements
- Walks around furniture lifting one foot and stepping sideways (cruising)
- Rolls over from front to back
- Can lift head when lying on tummy and move it from side to side
- Moves arms and legs, arms more than legs and chuckles when played with
- Grasps and shakes hand toys
- Kicks legs vigorously, one leg then the other
- Stands alone well
- Sits with, and then without, support
- Walks well
- Pulls self up to standing against furniture and can lower self back down again
- Walks with shorter steps and legs closer together, no longer needs to hold arms up for balance.

Sources of movement statements: (DCSF, 2008; Kyla Boyce, 2009).

In the past it was thought that the speed at which children passed through milestones was due to maturation rates that were genetically influenced and this could not be externally influenced. Smith et al. (2003) refer to this genetic predisposition as the 'blue print' for growth. Just as discussed above in reference to early brain growth the view on the role of genetics in maturation has now been re-evaluated so that the influence of environmental experience is also considered. Gallahue and Ozmun (2006) argue that it is erroneous to conclude that the maturational factors alone will ensure the development of movement and that a wide variety of meaningful movement experiences are necessary to help children refine their skills. Papalia et al. (2006) discuss how the infant and the environment form an interconnected system and that development has interacting causes. These authors also discuss the child's motivation as an additional contributory causational factor for movement as well as opportunities presented in the surrounding environment. Papalia et al. (2006) use the work of Thelen (1995) to evidence this. Thelen discusses the walking reflex or stepping movements a baby makes when held upright with the feet touching a surface. They discuss how this reflex gradually disappears in the fourth month of life but will often be reproduced after this time if young children are held in warm water. Thelen points to the environmental conditions and motivational factors that have promoted this stepping movement.

Opportunities to move – the child's viewpoint

The arguments expressed above demonstrate how providing opportunities to move are important for development. However, it would appear that some of the things we do to our children might prevent his/her from happening. For instance, children are placed in baby walkers despite evidence suggesting that they might actually inhibit the development of independent locomotion. David et al. (2003) discuss research on the use of baby walkers. In a study of over 170 children, those children whose parents placed them in a baby walker were less independently mobile than those who were not. These babies also tended to have more accidents.

Understanding developmental milestones and combining this with an acknowledgement of what the world might look like from a young child's point of view might encourage the development of more opportunities to move. Realization that a child with limited movement is virtually dependent on their supporting adult changing their environment can be a powerful force. For a very young child who can only lie on their back or roll on to their front, understanding what their view is might be is useful. A child who is on their back for long periods of time might therefore only really be able to see the ceiling or objects that are placed in his/her view point; providing objects above the child in different locations might encourage that individual to reach out and grasp them, thus encouraging independent movement. Changing the child's orientation is also important. Sitting a child in a bouncy chair can completely alter what a child can see or maybe reach out and touch. Lifting a child up and down so that they can see and try and touch their carer's face from a different perspective changes the child's viewpoint once more. Taking a child outside and letting them feel the air on their face or letting them touch the grass can provide new experiences and add to desire to move. Providing interesting materials that require the use of the 'pincer grasp' (the ability to grasp items between the thumb and the index finger) might produce the desire to achieve this developmental milestone.

Practical task

How can your educational setting's environment be further improved in order to encourage the desire to move in very young children with limited mobility.

Keeping safe

When children are learning to move safety can become an issue. Indeed 'keeping safe' is frequently highlighted in the 'movement and space' aims and objectives in the *Practice Guide for the Early Years Foundation Stage* (DCSF, 2008). The emphasis on staying safe has been consolidated in recent years by the Every Child Matters (DfES, 2003a) agenda which lists 'staying' safe as one of its central aims. For very young children it is the responsibility of caring adults to keep children safe. Very young children who cannot articulate their thoughts and feelings rely on adults to create an environment that is appropriate for them to explore. There is now a plethora of information provided by local and central government bodies that can inform parents, childminders and educational establishments on how to keep environments safe. For instance, Ofsted (2008) stipulate that all childminders must carry out annual risk assessments on the safety of their home. Child minders must ensure that they have a relevant First Aid qualification, they must check that their home is suitably protected against the dangers of alcohol, drugs, smoke and unsuitable medications and that equipment used by children complies with safety standards.

It would be foolhardy to ignore relevant safety measures but this awareness needs to balanced with allowing children enough freedom to take risks in order to develop physically. Garrick (2004) outlines how society and its concern with safety has led to the over-protection of children which increasingly limits them physically. Informal observations have certainly shown how parents are concerned that children should avoid taking risks in case of accident; it seems it is easier to stop a child from participating rather than letting them have a go. Palmer (2006) explores this theme in some detail. For instance, she discusses the 'Back to Sleep' campaign that advises that babies should be put to sleep on their backs to avoid Sudden Infant Death syndrome. Palmer tracks how this has been linked to an increase in dyspraxia for children who do not get adequate time lying on their fronts which results on them being slow to lift themselves on their arms and then to move via crawling. She also discusses how older children, who need to work off excess energy, increasingly spend time using technology watching other people exercise. Finally, she discusses the trend of parents who are worried about the effect of the sun and prefer to keep their children indoors on hot days. While noting the need for safety, Palmer calls for a return to a more measured view to safeguarding children so that they can obtain sufficient opportunities for good development.

Case study

One of my own earliest memories is exploring the space around my home. I can remember the different textures on the ground around my house. I can remember sitting on the back door step, this was made of smooth, cold concrete, this was the patio area. I can recall the feeling of the grass under the apple tree at the end of the garden, this often had twigs and leaf litter under it and it was prickly underfoot. I can remember the smooth wooden feel of the slide. I can recall the feel of the ground around the drive way, this was bumpy and ever so slightly painful to walk on but this did not really deter me from doing so although using the curb at the side was occasionally a more appealing option. I can remember the look of the house next door, I can visualize the location of the steps at the end of the garden, where I would observe the house backing on to ours. The type of fencing that separated the two houses was the type from which you could easily get splinters.

⇨

Case study—Cont'd

I left this house when I was 5 years old, this is over 30 years ago, but early experiences and plenty of opportunities to move have left a very good mental image of the area.

Reflection for early career professional

- Think about your early experiences, can you remember what opportunities you were given for physical development, how does this compare to the opportunities children receive today?
- From the time I spent exploring this area around my home, I must have made a very good mental map of this environment – are children in your care given enough time to be able to achieve this?

Reflection for leader/manager

- Due to the fact that I can remember so many textures underfoot I must of spent much of the time outside without shoes, consider the health and safety implications here; how would this sort of situation would be viewed today?

Movement and space from 3 to 5 years of age

During this age phase children are likely to be refining their physical skills in the home, in a pre-school facility or more formally in a Foundation Stage setting. By the end of the Foundation Stage children will be assessed on their physical development skills. The Early Learning Goals (DCFS, 2008) for the curriculum area 'Movement and Space' are as follows:

- Move with confidence, imagination and safety
- Move with control and coordination
- Travel around, under, over and through balancing and climbing equipment
- Show awareness of space, of themselves and of others

During this age range children need to continue to master control of their movement skills in three main ways:

- Gross Motor Skills – this is managing control of large body movements that involve large muscles, for example, bending, twisting pushing and pulling. Because of patterns of development children will achieve management of many of their gross motor skills before fine motor skills.

Photograph 1.2 Gross Motor Skill Development (© P. Hopkins)

- Loco motor skills – these are linked to gross motor skills but involves the body moving in some way e.g. running, jumping, hopping, skipping.
- Fine Motor Skills – physical skills that involve small muscles and eye hand coordination (Papalia et al., 2006). Many young children will be slower to develop the ability to draw, cut, colour in and stick than large movement actions. These sorts of activities require management of the muscles in the wrist and hand, the more mature the child's wrist and finger development the more successful the child will be and their hand will not tire so quickly. Children who might appear off task, or lack concentration, might simply be experiencing a lack of development in the required muscles for successful completion of these sorts of tasks (Whitebread, 1996).

The importance of movement

Movement is imperative for young children of this age. Movement not only allows children to develop physically but holistically. The Early Years Foundation Stage (DCSF, 2008) recognizes the importance of movement not only in the areas of 'learning and development' but also via

- the commitment that describes 'active' learning which requires children to be mentally and *physically* engaged in learning,
- the commitment of 'learning environments' which emphasises the creation of an outdoor area that allows children to use their senses, and be physically active and exuberant.

To deny children the experience of movement activity will have global consequences for all other areas of development. There is currently high value placed on 'academic' subjects in a bid to raise standards in literacy and numeracy. As children move into Key Stage 1 the emphasis to achieve is concentrated by the requirement to make nationally shared summative assessments of children in number, reading, writing, speaking and listening. As a result early literacy and numeracy skills are valued with parents being very concerned about the development of these attributes. To misunderstand the importance of physical development and movement might have a direct consequence for the development of early literacy/numeracy skills. Due to patterns of development children need to build up strength in their large muscles before being able to develop the finer motor skills required for pencil control. Experience of movement is also vital in helping children make sense of the world. Athey (1990) developed Piaget's (1896–1980) notion of schemas or repeated patterns of behaviour. Through movement children might begin to make sense of themselves, properties of objects and that of shape and space. Lindon (2005) argues that without this understanding of schemas adults might interpret some activities of children as pointless or time wasting. Different types of schema might include the following

- trajectory – interest in things that go up and down and along and back
- rotation
- enclosure
- enveloping and containing

- connecting – joining things together in different ways
- transporting – interest in moving things in different ways (Athey, 1990).

To be able to fathom abstract ideas children need experience of different types of movement. For instance, to be able to understand the concept of 'on top' and 'underneath' children need to do this physically. To be able to understand the proportions of space and depth children need to experience this feeling via enclosure and enveloping and containing.

Case study

A teacher was delivering the topic of 'exploration' with a foundation stage class. The teacher was keen to create a role-play corner on jungles. She set up a very imaginative area with pretend trees, jungle animals, equipment that might be taken on a journey to a jungle, books, cameras, materials to write down information and dressing up clothes which might be suitable for exploration. The building that the class was based in was quite old and curious in shape; in the role-play corner there was a recess in the wall (shaped like an old fireplace) with a ledge that could be sat on. The teacher had imaginatively placed camouflaged netting material over the front of the space and attached soft animals to it that could be taken off and played with. The teacher said the role-play area could be used in any way but the children should not untie the netting and go in the space behind it. Although the role-play area was very much enjoyed by the children, they had the best fun by undoing the netting and trying to sit in the space behind it. The teacher was at a loss as to why this should be and decided to read more about behaviours of children to identify possible reasons. A colleague recommended that she read about types of behaviour and schema and this helped the teacher suddenly realize why the children might be acting in this manner. The corner was then adapted so that the children could take advantage of this readymade hidey hole that offered so many play opportunities.

Practical task

Spend time observing young children playing, can you identify any possible schema attached to their movement.

Outdoor movement

Photograph 1.3 Outdoor Physical Play Area (photograph taken by Emma Jordan)

While children in the Foundation Stage might meet opportunities to move in formal PE lessons they also need be physically active throughout the day. The implementation of the Early Years Foundation Stage (DCFS, 2008) with its emphasis on active learning and use of the outdoor environment has ensured that there is a concentration on activity and a reinvigoration of the use of outside space. Young children need space to develop their motor skills in a well planned outdoor space. Bilton (2004) argues that outdoors is the best place to learn through movement and to develop physically. She advises that to learn through movement there needs to be enough space to move, do and find out; enclosed spaces can result in overcrowding and aggressive behaviour particularly in boys. Movement outside gives children a different sense of space, they need to able to feel space not just around them but above them as well. Bilton (1998) advises that learning outdoors will give children the experience of large muscle movements which are used when, for example, swinging from a bar or digging un the mud. This strengthening of the arm muscles will in turn enable smaller muscles to be used when drawing or writing.

Through time outside children will experience learning about balance, coordination and body awareness. Bilton (2004) advocates that this should not be achieved through structured fitness lessons but through a 'whole body approach' where physical activity pervades all tasks. The Early Years Foundation Stage (DCFS, 2008) also recommends this approach but additionally advocates that much physical learning should be developed via spontaneous play opportunities This is supported by Papalia et al. (2006) who argue that young children develop best when they can be active at an appropriate maturational level during unstructured free play.

The variety and type of outdoor provision can therefore greatly enhance opportunities for play and the development of movement. The use of equipment and apparatus is discussed later in this book. It is worth noting, however, different types of play and different equipment arrangements can encourage physical development. Mitsuru(1992) determined three types of play in relation to the use of play structures.

Functional play: when children use a play structure for the purpose it was designed, for example, a child sitting on a swing and asking someone to push them or learning how to gain height themselves.

Technical play: children will explore the potential of a structure to invent new ways of moving. For instance, children might kneel on a swing when playing on it or they might lie over the swing seat on their tummies and experience the sensation of rocking back and forth in a different position.

Social play: involves using the play structure but not in the way it was intended. The play structure is merely the basis for the play. For instance, the swing now acts as a separating structure between which children play throwing and catching, part of the game being that the children have to throw a ball over the swing seat and between the chains.

Mitsuru (1992) argues that equipment provision should allow for all the above types of play; technical and social play make for situations where children can acquire a greater range of motor skills, take more risks in a safe environment and produce even more complex games. This can be linked to exemplars of general good educational scenarios in the Practice Guidance for the Early Years Foundation Stage (DCFS, 2008). This document suggests that more effective types of play activity occur when children take ownership of an activity and 'subvert' it to a different purpose than intended. Practitioners should be aware of these different roles of play so that they can make informed decisions about the type of movement they plan for and allow, which in turn might encourage the initiation of more complex movements.

Case study

James, Sophie and Harry were playing outside at their educational establishment. They were playing at the playhouse area. The playhouse was a wooden structure which was raised about 1.5 metres off the ground, it looked as if it was standing on stilts. The entrance to the house was reached via a small step ladder that led to a balcony at the front. James, Sophie and Harry often played together at the house in different ways. One of their favourite games was when the adult in charge had rigged up a sheet around the supporting stilts in order to make a shelter underneath the house itself. The children would spend a lot of time running in and out of this improvised shelter and would often take out the play equipment provided in the house to play with in this shelter. They would pretend to cut and serve food and pour out drinks using a tea set. Much time was also spent fashioning an operational make-shift doorway with bits of string that could be attached to the sheet. Other times the children would wiggle and wind themselves through the open rungs of the steps leading up to the house. A really good game was to jump off the top of the steps onto the ground. At times they would jump of the slightly higher balcony and see how far each child could travel. As the year progressed and the children grew they liked to climb on top of the house to sit astride the pitched roof, there they liked to sit and talk to each other.

Reflection for early career professional

- What sort of physical skills are the children refining in this case study?
- How would you deal with the health and safety issues presented in this case study without feeling that you were limiting the children?
- The children in this case study sat on top of the house. Maude (2001) argues that play spaces should provide high places where children feel they can look down on the action. Why should children want to do this?

Reflection for leader/manager

- Is your large play equipment used in different ways so that the children can challenge their physical abilities?
- Does this case study demonstrate different types of play as detailed above by Mitsuru (1992)?

Movement in an indoor environment

As outlined above children need the opportunity to be physical in an unstructured manner. It might be argued that this sort of activity might best take place when children play outside. However, the 'principle' Enabling Environments in the Practice Guidance for the Early Years Foundation Stage (DCFS, 2008) states that children should be allowed sufficient space for energetic play both indoors and outdoors.

Wetton (1997) argues that children need to be able to run, climb and involved in rough and tumble activities. Wetton believes that preschools, in particular, were once places where children could practise all their physical skills but states that while the outdoor space might allow this, the indoor environment is now too limited to pre National Curriculum (DFEE and QCA, 1999) fine motor coordination activities and that the nearest children get to exercising their gross motor skills is in role-play corners or when using large building blocks. Wetton (1997) calls for more energetic play opportunities to be provided indoors and suggests that at the very least the indoor requirement for gross motor and loco motor play are provided through:

- access to an indoor climbing frame
- access to playing with toys with wheels
- access to large building blocks
- the right to move through an indoor space without restriction
- a space for teacher directed activities
- a space for rough and tumble play

Photograph 1.4 Rough and Tumble (© P. Hopkins)

The last requirement, in the bulleted points listed on the previous page, maybe the most difficult for practitioners to organize due to the current perception of rough and tumble play. Informal research reveals that rough and tumble play is somewhat frowned upon by parents who are concerned about children hurting themselves. This sort of activity may appear unseemly or pointless. Parents can also confuse their own past narrative of what is deemed to be appropriate behaviour, they may have been taught that to be 'seen and not heard' to 'sit still and not fidget' is the best model of producing a 'good' child. Rough and tumble play may appear to be out of control and indirectly deem the parents to be ineffective in their approach to child rearing. Online parental discussion boards commonly have questions from concerned parents about whether to allow rough and tumble play. Parents can also link this sort of play with aggression and worry about the onset of a bullying environment. However, children do need to be able to move freely and engage in physical play. During this type of activity children are testing out their physical and motor skills and also taking risks. In fact, Jarvis (2006) presents a powerful argument for the place of this type of movement stating that the creation of rough and tumble play opportunities put children into authentic situations where they can simultaneously practice spontaneous, autonomous, competitive and cooperative interaction, developing not only physical skills, but also many of the complex social skills that fundamentally underpin adult life. Rough and tumble play can, in fact, help children know the difference between what constitutes cooperative play and what is unacceptable aggression.

Greenland (2006) also discusses indoor movement and draws our attentions to the importance of learning through the senses. In particular she discusses two senses related to movement:

- The proprioceptive sense – the position of our body parts in relation to one another
- The vestibular sense – the sense of movement and the relationship to the ground.

Greenland (2006) states that without these senses being developed a child might find it hard to coordinate their movements, balance or formulate a sense of spatial awareness. These senses are developed by particular access to floor play on the tummy and backs, belly crawling, crawling, spinning, tipping, falling and tilting. Greenland (2006) discusses how some nurseries have started to develop their indoor area so that table top activities are placed on the floor so that children have 'tummy time'. She discusses other nurseries who have set aside whole movement afternoons where spaces are provided just for spontaneous, movement play.

Case study

Three-year old Rosie was investigating a series of interconnecting play tunnels provided in the indoor environment at her pre-school. The tunnel was dark blue and therefore it provided a rather dark and enclosed space. Rosie had been reticent about going through the tunnel for a number of days. She spent time peering into one end and running to the other end and looking in. She would also talk to play mates who were in the tunnel from one end. Eventually with some encouragement from a supporting adult Rosie was persuaded to wriggle through the tunnels. Having overcome her initial reluctance she gradually went through the tunnels over and over again and she really enjoyed this activity. She liked to take toys into the tunnel with her and bring them out the other side.

Reflection for early career professional

- What skills is Rosie learning here, is she developing physical development skills or other skills as well?
- Why do children appear to repeat activities over and over again?
- How could Rosie's play have been extended?
- Can you make any links between this case study and some of the themes and principles advocated in the Practice Guidance for the Early Years Foundation Stage (DCSF, 2008)?

Reflection for leader/manager

- Does your indoor provision have enough space set aside for the development of gross and loco motor skills?

As well as giving opportunities for unstructured play in order to develop physical skills, the principle 'active learning' in the Practice Guidance for the Early Years Foundation Stage (DCFS, 2008) states that children also learn through planned physical challenges. By planning for an integrated, active approach to the curriculum many activities will promote a range of skills, physical skills will be developed alongside social, emotional and cognitive attributes.

Case study

Joe was playing with an electronic mat with a supporting adult. The mat had footprints on it that were numbered from one to ten. Every time a footprint was stepped on an accompanying sound would be triggered. Stepping on the footprints in different combinations would result in different sounds being triggered. Joe enjoyed this mat and was often observed playing with it so some activities were designed around it for him. A teaching assistant used the mat to encourage movement and also develop the child's understanding of number. She asked Joe to jump on certain numbers, she then asked him to step on all the numbers in order from one to ten. Joe extended this activity by hopping from one number to the next. The assistant asked Joe to move backwards tracing the numbers from ten to one while counting backwards with him. Joe also spent time balancing on certain numbers and seeing how far his stride would reach and how many numbers he might step across in one go. Joe enjoyed stepping on different numbers in order to create simple 'tunes' from the different sounds.

Reflection for early career professional

- What areas of the curriculum is Joe developing?

Reflection for leader/manager

- How might this activity be extended to further Joe's development of
  - gross motor skills
  - his understanding of number
  - his understanding of ICT.

The next case study detailed below demonstrates how formal movement lessons can also be used to enhance the whole curriculum. Movement in this scenario might be used to consolidate abstract skills and concepts being taught in other areas of learning.

Case study

A foundation stage class had been studying Shape, Space and Measures; they had been working on the recognition of 2D shape. The teacher had been looking for an active approach to this area of learning and she used a PE lesson to reinforce conceptual understanding. After an initial warm-up the teacher started the lesson by asking the children to work in small groups. In their groups the children had to collectively arrange their bodies so that they formed various 2D shapes like squares and triangles. She then extended the lesson by giving each group a large piece of elastic that was joined together at each end. The children had to arrange themselves inside the elastic to make 2D shapes that were called out by the teacher. The children were also able to think of fairly advanced concepts using this approach For instance; the teacher introduced the concepts of regular and irregular shape. Finally ideas of symmetry in shape were also considered.

Reflection for early career professional

- What areas of the curriculum is this class accessing?
- What other mathematical concepts might be addressed and reinforced via a physical education lesson?

Reflection for leader/manager

- How might this activity be further extended?

Transition to Key Stage 1 (5 to 7 years of age)

As children transfer from the Early Years Foundation Stage to Key Stage 1 movement becomes more formalized via the PE curriculum. Children will meet the majority of their movement development through activities that centre on dance, gymnastics and games.

By the end of Key Stage 1, The National Curriculum (DfEE and QCA, 1999) requires children in dance to

- use movement imaginatively, responding to stimuli, including music and performing basic skills

- change the rhythm, speed, level and direction of their movements
- create and perform dances using simple movement patterns including those from different times and cultures
- express and communicate ideas and feelings.

In games activities in Key Stage 1 the National Curriculum (DfEE and QCA, 1999) requires children to be able to

- travel with, send and receive a ball and other equipment in different ways
- develop these skills for simple net, striking/fielding and invasion type games
- play simple, competitive net, striking/fielding and invasion type games that they and other have made, using simple tactics for attacking and defending.

Finally, the National Curriculum (DfEE and QCA, 1999) requires young children studying gymnastics to

- perform basic skills in travelling, being still, finding space and using it safely, both on the floor and using apparatus
- develop the range of their skills and actions
- choose and link skills and actions in short movement phrases
- create and perform short, linked sequences that show clear beginnings, middles and ends and have contrasts in direction, level and speed.

As children develop and mature the emphasis in physical development moves from initial mastery of basic movement to practising and refining skills. No longer do children have trouble standing or jumping but they need to be physically active in order to develop their ability to refine skills to catch or hit a tennis ball, for example. Gallahue and Ozmun (2006) state that complex movements performed by professional sports persons or dancers are merely more highly elaborated forms of fundamental movement developed and combined with one another at a more sophisticated level of functioning. These fundamental movements are made up from three main categories:

- Locomotion – for example, methods of travelling
- Manipulation – for example, catching and kicking
- Stability, for example, bending, stretching, twisting and turning.

The development of these skills is associated with a term called motor fitness. Motor fitness is said to be the quality of performance of a fitness task (Gallahue, 1982). Motor fitness is made up of five main components:

- Coordination
- Speed
- Agility
- Power
- Balance

Having a understanding of what constitutes good 'motor fitness' will help practitioners to make better assessments of a child's progress in physical development. Indeed, having good subject knowledge of quality of movement will make for better delivery of the PE curriculum. Poor subject knowledge and teacher under-confidence are long-standing and often reported themes among the teaching profession in PE. Wetton (1997) comments on the apprehension of practitioners when delivering games lessons; she notes that they often 'fear' this area of the curriculum as they might teach in a way that is deemed 'old fashioned' or that a technique might be incorrectly explained. Macfadyen and Osbourne (2000) also note feelings of inadequacy. Mawer (1999) discusses the restrictive range of teaching styles used when delivering the PE curriculum noting the paucity of those who used more sophisticated and constructivist teaching approaches. Giving educationalists knowledge of how movement can be broken down can give them greater confidence when analysing what makes for quality movement and consequently help in their assessment of children. As such, it is worth detailing the work of Rudolf Laban (1947) dancer and choreographer who worked in Europe in the 1930s and 1940s. Laban produced a form of movement notation called *Labanotation* and the Laban Movement Analysis. The movement analysis, comprising of four main categories, can increase awareness of how to ensure progression in the quality of movement.

Body awareness

Being aware of what the body is doing and how parts are connected, this might include actions by the whole body, parts of the body and shapes the body can make. An easy way to remember this is to ask: 'what' is the body doing?'

Space

This deals with where the body moves, it might concern use of different levels, directions and pathways. A simple way to remember this is to ask: 'where' the body is moving?

Effort

This concerns the dynamics of a movement and is the quality that I have observed pre-service teachers find most difficult to grasp. Effort concerns the timing and forcefulness of a movement; this gives the movement interest and texture. Flow is also connected with effort; free flow movement would be continuous movement, while bound flow is the opposite of this. This quality is usually most associated with dance and gymnastic activities but can equally be applied to sports.

Relationships

This concept is defined by what certain body parts are doing in relation to the rest of the body, it might also be associated with the relationship of a person with a partner, group or the rest of the class.

Practical task

Look at the statements listed below. Which statements promote body awareness, relationships, effort or space? Can some statements be placed under more than one heading?

- throw the ball as hard as you can
- refine your movements with a partner and perform them together
- uncurl like a blossoming flower, can you make your movement continuous? Don't stop moving until the music ends.
- move around the hall freely, when I shake the tambourine move in a different direction
- move around the hall freely, when I shake the tambourine use your body to move on a different level
- scamper around the hall like a mouse, now can you glide like a giraffe
- travel with your partner using a roll and jump
- balance on your tiptoes
- point to your elbow, now point to your shoulder
- 'make your body copy the movements I am making'
- perform a balance with a partner where you use your combined weight to sustain it.

Case study

Year 2 were participating in a dance lesson. The lesson complemented their topic theme of light and dark, this lesson was entitled 'shadows'. The lesson began with a warm up activity where the teacher played a game of 'Simon Says' with the children. The class had to copy the teacher's exact movements. The warm up continued with an exercise on mirroring movement. The children had to find a partner, one child was asked to volunteer to act as a mirror image to the other. The children had to concentrate on copying the movements of each other performing a familiar routine like brushing hair or washing their faces. The teacher encouraged the children to work slowly so as to let them closely observe and imitate actions. Praise was given to those children who were executing this activity with success; one pair also demonstrated their actions to the rest of the class. The class talked about the meaning of the term 'mirror' and shadows. In the main part of the lesson the teacher introduced a short poem on shadowing composed of four short lines. She read the poem to the class and asked the children to work in pairs where one person acted as the other child's shadow. The children had to devise movement for each line of the poem. The poem used language which gave opportunities for the class to create a movement vocabulary that required them to uncurl and curl up again, twist and turn, roll, travel and drop to the floor. Giving the children time to produce a movement for each line of the poem helped to give them a simple structure making the narrative of creating a dance an easily accessible task. The teacher gave the children an opportunity to practice each line of the poem and then required them to perform the dance in completion. When performing the dance the teacher split the class in half and asked some children to sit and observe the rest of the class performing. The children watching the performance were then asked to evaluate their peers in order to articulate how the performances could be improved. Once all the performances were complete the children spent the last part of the lesson refining their dances, during this time the teacher asked the children to make all their movements sustained and continuous while she read the poem in order that the dances might flow. The class concluded with a period of cooling down before the children returned to the classroom.

Practical task

Apply Laban's movement analysis to this lesson; were the four categories of body awareness, space, effort and relationships catered for?

Reflection for early career professional

- Identify elements of good planning and practice in this dance lesson
- How could the lesson be further improved?
- What other areas of the curriculum could be developed from this lesson?

Reflection for leader/manager

- Do your staff have sufficient subject knowledge to be able to extend and progress the development of movement in your educational establishment?

Recent developments in physical education

When the Government green paper 'Every Child Matters' (DfES, 2003a) proposed 'staying healthy' as one of its five central tenets the curriculum area of physical education was given renewed emphasis after a period of draught. This dearth of interest was caused by an overemphasis on subjects like literacy and numeracy which had associated SAT's (Standard Attainment Tests) attached to them. In recent years there has been a desire to increase the time given to physical education and a change in the way it is accessed in the curriculum. In 2002 the Labour government launched the PE, School Sport and Club Links (PESSCL) strategy to be delivered by the Department for Education and Skills (DfES, 2002) and the Department for Culture, Media and Sport (DCMS). The overall objective was to enhance the up take of sporting opportunities by 5–16 year olds. The aim of this initiative was to increase the percentage of school children in England who spend a minimum of 2 hours each week on high quality PE and school sport within and beyond the curriculum to 75 per cent by 2006 (DfES, 2003b). This target was then extended to children being involved in at least 4 hours of sport per week by 2010 (DfES, 2004). This initiative not only extended curriculum time but paved the way for school clubs to offer an increased range of activities. It also allowed sports coaches to teach parts of the curriculum that were previously delivered by the teacher. Schools are currently engaged in offering a range of sporting activities that may have been previously inaccessible. Specialist sports coaches are now more and more involved in the delivery of the curriculum. While there are many positive aspects to this development, it might also have a long-term negative of further de-skilling the primary teacher who may no longer be involved in the delivery of the PE curriculum for long periods of time. Moreover, although coaches might be better placed to teach sports skills development, this has to be balanced with an understanding of pedagogy and effective learning strategies, this might not always a reality.

While the initiatives referred to above have given physical education more emphasis there now needs to be recognition of the role of movement as a means of learning across the whole curriculum. When children progress from the Foundation Stage they are still met with a more structured curriculum where opportunities to move can be limited. Children in this age phase have to meet the demands of the literacy and numeracy strategies and may be required to conform to a more traditional notion of what makes for good learning. Time spent sitting on the carpet can lengthen. For children, especially for those with summer birthdays and who might only just be 5 years of age, this can be a challenge and result in difficulties in paying attention. This factor combined with pressure to fit in a busy curriculum results in some afternoon playtimes being made optional or indeed in Key Stage 2 being omitted all together. This does not make for a good learning environment; children need plenty of breaks in order to optimise concentration periods.

The problems associated with the demands of early onset of formalized learning are now being recognized. Smith (2003) in his extremely popular and accessible text '*Accelerated Learning in Practice*' argues that children should not be 'slumped' behind desks for long periods. Smith advocates that physical activity promotes learning. Santrock (2007) states that children become more fatigued by long periods of sitting than by running, jumping or bicycling. Bruce (2004) asserts that the development of learning is 'hindered' and even 'damaged' if young children are placed in classrooms that require numerous paper and pencil exercises and long periods of sitting still. For young children, sitting still may be the hardest action for them to achieve (Lindon, 2005). Pupils need sufficient time, space and planned opportunities during which they can explore and develop their physical skills. Gradually it is being acknowledged, particularly by Rose (2009) in the *Independent Review of the Primary Curriculum*, that the good practices of active and physical learning, exemplified by the EYFS, should be applied to Key Stage 1. As a result, initiatives are occurring in school that require children to be physically active outside the PE lesson. For instance, movement programmes that concentrate on the daily application of a set of movement techniques that promote coordination and rhythm are currently extremely popular in schools.

Case studies

Scenario 1

Year 1 were undertaking some daily movement activity. They were following a program of movement that involved copying a person moving; the program was displayed via an interactive whiteboard. The task for the day was centred on stretching and curling. All children participated well and the teacher also joined in the experience. The teacher raised the quality of the action by her use of language. Noticing the children were not particularly stretching out she started to add phrases

Photograph 1.5 Curling up Like Mice (photograph by Lindy Nahmad-Williams)

like 'can you stretch your fingers so they touch the ceiling', 'can you make yourself grow more', 'I can feel my muscles really stretching,' 'can you hold your position without wobbling', 'I can see you are really still.' She also allowed some children to demonstrate their stretching to others and subsequently gave praise and asked the children how else they might make their movement better. She encouraged the children to curl up so they could be as minute as mice.

Scenario 2

Year 1 were undertaking some daily movement activity. They were following a program of movement that involved copying a person moving; the program was displayed via interactive whiteboard. The task for today was centred on stretching but involved the children making circular motions with their arms. The class had been rather restless that morning, it was the start of the day and the activity program was commenced as the children came into class. The teacher was not initially watching the children as she was involved with parents at the classroom door. As the task progressed the children became engaged in the activity. They started to listen to the music and the class moved in time to the rhythm. The class quietened and enjoyed the rhythmic activity, they moved and breathed in unison, they became caught up in the calmness and atmosphere created by the music. The activity finished and the class sat down quietly on the carpet where their teacher greeted them and quietly congratulated the children on such a good start to the day.

When considering the above case studies might appear, on initial reflection, that the first scenario might offer the better practice. However, I would argue that both case studies are worthwhile learning experiences, what is important is that the teacher involved was sufficiently aware to know why and how they were both good opportunities for learning. In the first scenario the teacher used her knowledge of the power of language, modelling and evaluation to create the best from the experience. In the second, the teacher used movement for a different purpose. The activity was used to 'calm' the class and she understood that at times it is valuable to let the children experience the joy of movement for itself without interruption from a well meaning adult.

Reflection for early career professional

- Find out if your educational establishment offers a movement programme like the one described above.
- If you already deliver sessions like this think about how you can apply your language skills to make for the best types of learning opportunities.

Case studies—Cont'd

Reflection for leader/manager

- Movement programmes as described above are often commenced with gusto. Consider how enthusiasm and high quality learning situations can be sustained over a long period of time.

In addition to extra input of movement in the daily routine of a class there should perhaps also be a renewed focus on using movement to access the whole curriculum. Doherty and Brennan (2008) refer to this as 'education through movement' and describe this aspect of teaching as the use of physical activities as a means to achieve educational aims that may not be intrinsic to those activities. Physical education is a wider process of general education, by keeping children engaged in activities that are static and passive much of the joy of learning can be lost.

Case study

Year 1 were studying Hinduism, particularly Divali. The class had been read the story of Rama and Sita and then they had been split into groups to tackle tasks in a carousel of activities. One of the activities involved sequencing the story of Rama and Sita by placing a series of laminated cards in order. Another activity involved some of the children writing and drawing the practices associated with Divali, the final task involved the children making creating Rangoli patterns. During this activity the children studied pattern, symmetry and colours associated with these types of design. The children were able to choose a geometric design to which they could add coloured sands, coloured rice and other bright materials. The children were given a free reign to their design but were asked to try and place materials in a pattern. The task actually sounds fairly simplistic but it took much patience and concentration to apply PVA glue correctly to their design and also then place fine sands in the correct position in order to produce a pattern. It took great control of the chidrens' fine motor skills and coordination to actually control the materials appropriately. Much sand was spilt in the process despite the children being on task and sustaining their concentration. The children were asked to reflect on their work as it progressed, some children asked to start their work again which the teacher permitted.

This task required a variety of physical skills to be applied by the children particularly in the area of precision and coordination. Tasks like this can sometimes be seen as having a lesser value to activities that involve literacy and numeracy. In this case, however, the teacher had a good understanding of how this cross-curricular approach would develop a multitude of skills and that tasks that might at first appear less cognitively challenging actually demanded a great deal of effort by the children. She also knew controlling and manipulating the application of materials might also indirectly benefit pencil control and coordination.

Reflection for early career professional

- Do you think the teacher was right to let the children start their work again?
- Do you design cross-curricular activities that develop an active approach that require the use of both gross and fine motor skills?

Reflection for leader/manager

- Do your staff and support assistants have enough understanding of physical development and pedagogy to sufficiently place equal value on a range of activities apart from literacy and numeracy?

Conclusion

Young children need to be active. Children need to be given opportunities to acquire, practise and refine their physical skills. Practitioners need to have an understanding of milestones for acquiring physical skills and how to progress, extend and assess the quality of movement demonstrated by children in their care. Children need to be given plenty of opportunities to move in both structured and unstructured situations. Creating opportunities for physical development through play will help children gain control of their bodies. Children need to be given opportunities for movement both indoors and outside. Children need to be able to take risks in their movement in order to extend their bodies; challenging movement opportunities should be planned for by practitioners. Children learn best when they can use their physicality and have an active approach to learning. Movement helps to not only acquire physical skills but also to enhance and extend all other areas of the curriculum.

References

Athey, C. (1990) *Extending Thought in Young Children: A Parent Teacher Partnership.* London: Paul Chapman

Bilton, H. (1998) *Outdoor Play in the Early Years. Management and Innovation.* London: David Fulton Publishers

Bilton, H. (2004) *Playing Outside: Activities, Ideas and Inspiration for the Early Years.* London: David Fulton Publishers

Bruce, T. (2004) *Developing Learning in Early Childhood.* London: Sage

Cooper, L. (2008) What is Physical Development? in Johnston, J and Nahmad- Williams, L. (eds), *Early Childhood Studies.* Harlow: Pearson Education

DCSF. (2008) *Practice Guidance for the Early Years Foundation Stage: setting the standards for learning, development and care for children from birth to five.* London: Department for Children, Schools and Families

DFEE and QCA. (1999) *The National Curriculum.* London: Crown Copyright and QCA

DfES. (2003) Every Child Matters. Summary of Green Paper. Available from: *http://www.everychild-matters.gov.uk/_files/B889EFF62F56A9E4C69778A869B3DA44.pdf* (Accessed June 2009)

DfES. (2003) Learning Through PE and Sport. Available from: *http://www.teachernet.gov.uk/_doc/9441/20030707%20Learning%20through%20PE%20and%20sport.pdf* (Accessed June 2009)

DfES. (2004) Boost for School Sports. Available from: *http://www.teachernet.gov.uk/_doc/7989/boost-leaflet.pdf* (Accessed June 2009)

David, T., Goouch, K., Powell, S. and Abbot, L. (2003) Birth to Three Matters: A Review of the Literature. Available from: *http://www.standards.dcsf.gov.uk/eyfs/resources/downloads/rr444.pdf* (Accessed June 2009)

Doherty, J. and Brennan, P. (2008) *Physical Education and Development 3–11: A guide for teachers.* Oxon: Routledge Taylor and Francis Group

Gallahue, D. (1982) *Developmental Movement Experiences for Children.* New York: John Wiley and Sons, Inc

Gallahue, D. and Ozmun, J (2006) *Understanding Motor Development. Infants, Children, Adolescents, Adults* 6th edn. New York. McGraw-Hill

Garrick, R. (2004) *Playing Outdoors in the Early Years.* London: Continuum

Goddard Blythe, S (2005) Releasing Intelligence Through Movement. Available from: http://www.inpp.org.uk/ (Accessed June 2009)

Greenland, P. (2006). Physical Development, in Bruce, T (ed), *Early Childhood: A Guide for Students.* London: Sage

Jarvis, P. (2006). Rough and Tumble Play: Lessons in Life. *Evolutionary Psychology* 4, 330–46. Available from: *http://www.epjournal.net/filestore/ep043303462.pdf* (Accessed June 2009)

Kyla Boyce, R. N. (2009) Your Child Development and Behaviour Resources: A guide to information and support for parents. Available from: *http://www.med.umich.edu/yourchild/topics/devmile.htm* (Accessed June 2009)

Laban, R. and Lawrence F, C. (1947) *Effort*. London: MacDonald and Evans

Lindon, J. (2005) *Understanding Child Development. Linking Theory and Practice*. Abbingdon: Hodder Arnold

Macfadyen, T. and Osbourne, M. (2000) Teaching Games, in Bailey, R. and Macfadyen, T (eds), *Teaching Physical Education 5–11*. London: Continuum, pp. 13–55

Maude, P. (2001) *Physical Children, Active Teaching. Investigating Physical Literacy*. Buckingham. Open University Press

Mawer, M. (1999) Teaching Styles and Teaching Approaches in Physical Education: Research Developments, in Hardy, C and Mawer, M (eds), *Learning and Teaching in Physical Education*. Oxon: Routledge Falmer Taylor and Francis Group, pp. 83–104

Mitsuru, S. (1992) *Design of Children's Play Environments*. New York: McGraw-Hill

Ofsted. (2008) Requirements for the Childcare Register: Childminders and homecarers, a child care factsheet. Available from: *http://www.ofsted.gov.uk/content/download/6850/70425/file/Requirements%20for%20the%20Childcare%20Register%20-%20childminders%20and%20home%20childcarers%20-%20factsheet.doc.* (Accessed June 2009).

Palmer, S. (2006) *Toxic Childhood. How the modern world is damaging our children and what we can do about it*. Orion: London.

Papalia, D., Wendkos Olds, S. and Duskin Feldman, R. (2006). *A Child's World. Infancy Through Adolescence*. New York. McGraw Hill

Rose, J. (2009) Independent Review of the Primary Curriculum: Final Report. Available from: *http://publications.teachernet.gov.uk* (Accessed May 2009)

Santrock, J. (2007) *Child Development*. Boston: McGraw Hill

Smith, A. (2003) *Accelerated Learning in Practice*. Stafford: Network Educational Press Ltd

Smith, P., Cowie, H. and Blades, M. (2003) *Understanding Children's Development*. Oxford: Blackwell Publishing

Thelen, E. (1995) Motor Development: A new synthesis. *American Psychologist* 50, (2), 79–95

Wetton, P. (1997). *Physical education in the early years. (Teaching and learning in the first three years of school)*. London: Routledge

Whitebread, D. (1996) *Teaching and Learning in the Early Years*. London: Routledge

Health and Bodily Awareness

If we could give every individual the right amount of nourishment and exercise, not too little and not too much, we would have found the safest way to health (Hippocrates (460–357 BC)).

Introduction

There are a number of definitions of health and you may well have your own, but perhaps the most common is the one offered 60 years ago by the World Health Organisation as, 'a state of complete physical, mental and social well-being, and not merely the absence of disease or infirmity . . .' (WHO, 1948a). In the time since this definition, the right of each individual to health has been championed by many countries across the world and is integral to national and regional treaties on human rights, highlighting among other things, the availability of and access to services, conditions of living and nutritious eating (WHO, 1948b). Contemporary views about health still regard an absence of illness as important, but set more store on the wider social and cultural factors that impact on health. We now appreciate that the effects of the environment on children's health are considerable. Their immune systems are less mature than those of adults. They ingest and inhale greater amounts of air and water relative to their body size than adults and consequently are more vulnerable to associated contaminant risks. Children under five can ingest between 20 mg and 400 mg of soil daily when playing out of doors, putting their hands in their mouths and eating it. A common enough scenario in early years! When older children were asked about their ideas on what good and bad health meant in relation to the environment (HPA, 2009), their responses were quite revealing. We particularly like the punch line that good health is about being 'vibrant, alive, full of energy and having life on track' (HPA, 2009: 38).

Good health means	Bad health means
"exercise"	"lazy lifestyle"
"green spaces"	"negative effects of being
"clean fresh air"	in a smoky environment"
"good dental health"	"pollution"
"good mental health"	"depression"
"good home life and family values"	"stress"
"eating healthy – lots of fruit and vegetables"	"obesity linked to fast food and no exercise"

(Adapted from Young people's ideas on good and bad health and associated environmental factors. HPA., 2009).

Figure 2.1 Young people's views on good and bad health

The Early Years Foundation Stage (DCSF, 2008) considers health as 'an integral part of their (children's) emotional, mental, social, environmental and spiritual well-being and is supported by attention to these aspects' (Principle into Practice Card 1.4). It is around these areas and the relationship among them that gives a broader definition of health. The EYFS is threaded throughout this chapter, but at this point it is important to signal the four elements that support this definition of health and form this chapter – physical health, mental well-being, keeping safe and healthy eating.

Physical health (a broader definition than fitness) includes the growth and physical development of the body. Physical activity is 'a behaviour that occurs in a variety of forms and contexts, including free play, house chores, exercise, school physical education, and organized sport' (Malina et al., 2004: 6). Taking the population as a whole, children are the most active group. A number of factors influence physical activity levels and patterns in children. Biological factors, for example, mean that boys are more active generally than girls, that activity declines with age and that overweight children prefer activities of low intensity. Psychological factors identify the benefits of being active, possible barriers to being active, cues to exercise and personal knowledge about physical activity. There are social factors such as adult modelling and peer support to be considered and environmental factors such as the day of the week, the season, indoor and outdoor settings and competition from television and video games (Sallis, 1994). Healthy lifestyles begin in early childhood where attitudes towards and habits of exercise and the enjoyment that accompanies it begins. We want children to enjoy and see the value and benefits of physical activity in their lifestyle and have a commitment to it that stays with them for life. While there is consensus that physical activity is associated with many positive outcomes in childhood, providing accurate measures of just how active young children are, is no easy task. Current national guidelines (NICE, 2009) recommend that children do a minimum of 60 minutes of at least moderate-intensity physical activity each day. However, studies show that these levels are not being met by children and there are concerns from policy makers, parents and practitioners that this lack of activity is a contributory factor in the ever-increasing rise in childhood obesity figures. Children today are fatter than ever before and many lead unhealthy lifestyles. Serious health inequalities mean that the least advantaged in society are more likely to experience ill health throughout their lives (more of this later).

Mental health is often used synonymously with 'wellness' or 'well-being', and describes either a level of *cognitive* or *emotional well-being* or the absence of a *mental disorder*. Mental health is often overshadowed by an emphasis on physical health but the two actually sit side by side. The 1999 Mental Health Foundation publication Bright Futures defined children who are mentally healthy as being able to

- develop psychologically, emotionally, intellectually and spiritually
- initiate, develop and sustain mutually satisfying personal relationships

- use and enjoy solitude
- become aware of others and empathize with them
- play and learn
- develop a sense of right and wrong
- resolve (face) problems and setbacks and learn from them.

The *World Health Organization* (2007) eloquently defined mental health as 'a state of well-being in which the individual realizes his or her own abilities, can cope with the normal stresses of life, can work productively and fruitfully, and is able to make a contribution to his or her community.' This definition shows that *emotional* well-being is about living a full and *creative* life with flexibility to deal with life's challenges. Surely this is what we want for children everywhere. A good state of mental well-being is concerned with how children feel, think and behave and is fundamental to the quality of their lives. Its effects are certainly long lasting. We know that unhappy children can grow into unhappy adults. Conversely, children with good mental health achieve academically and make lasting relationships (Mental Health Foundation, 1999). From a growing body of research evidence, we now know more about the factors that impact upon young children's psychological health and well-being, and what can be done to positively influence this. We know, for example, that psychological well-being is affected both positively and negatively by a child's genetic make-up; parental influences and by peers, families and the wider community. What young children experience helps shape their mental health and therefore the experiences they have with childminders, in Children's Centres, schools and settings are crucial. They need to be welcoming and affirming places for every child. Unless a child feels healthy mentally, he/she will be unable to achieve optimum physical health and well-being.

Very much related to this, children need to feel **safe**. Children need security, stability and care that protects them from mistreatment and neglect, accidental injury, bullying, discrimination and anti-social behaviour (Ofsted, 2005). Children under 5 years of age are most likely to have an accident in the home, and boys are more at risk than girls. The cost of accidents to children in the home is estimated at over £200 million a year, but even more important are the physical and emotional costs of serious accidents which can leave permanent scarring and psychological trauma to the child and his/her family. An increasing focus on early development and care brings opportunities to keep children safe, to promote their health and well-being, and provide support to parents, carers and practitioners in their daily work with children in the different early years settings. Good diet and **nutrition** are fundamental to health throughout our lives. Food is a marker of social inclusion and very much at the heart of social interactions. Many of our special celebrations like birthdays, weddings and festivals involve children sharing in special meals with family and friends. We know that nutritional patterns are established early in a child's life, and that infancy and early childhood are important periods for the development of positive attitudes and habits towards nutrition that can impact on health later in life. Knowing about diet and nutrition and acting upon this information can help reduce the risk of many health problems. Although there is huge interest in obesity in childhood, the nutritional status of children covers both extremes of obesity and nutritional deficiency. Undernutrition (commonly known as malnutrition) refers to deficiency of energy or nutrients that impact upon a child's normal growth. Malnutrition is a serious issue in a number of poorly developed countries for children under five, which according to the World Health Organisation, corresponds to approximately 421 million children. Deficiencies in either diet or energy are associated with reduction in muscle mass, levels of physical activity and delays in motor development and also expose children to biological risks of infection and disease.

Photograph 2.1 A Safe Place to Play

Children growing up in England today are healthier than ever before. The previously common killer diseases of childhood (scarlet fever, diphtheria, measles and whooping cough) are now rare. In the period immediately after the Second World War, as many as 1 in 20 children would die in infancy. Nowadays, more children with serious illnesses and disabilities are surviving, and the UK infant mortality rate has fallen to 5 per 1,000 live births – less than a quarter of what it was at the beginning of the 1960s. New knowledge confirms that good diet and nutrition are fundamental to health throughout our lives and this along with the important role of physical activity in children's lives, is crucial in helping to reduce the risk of health problems such as obesity, CHD, some cancers and type-2 diabetes that are features of life in the 21st century. Children today benefit from better sanitation, a safe water supply and better air quality and from improvements to the built environment through higher-quality housing and safer transport. Most families are significantly better off and parents have higher expectations and aspirations for their children's health than they did before. With new advances in technology and neuroscience, our understanding of how babies' brains develop, of how early attachment between baby and mother influences a child's long-term emotional development has improved considerably. The past decade has seen continued improvements in young people and families' health services. These advances have been made possible through significant increased expenditure in health and education, and an emphasis on integrated services to respond quickly and effectively to the needs and expectations of children and their families. There has been significant investment in the children's workforce over the past decade. Children's Trusts have as part of their remit to improve outcomes of young children and reducing inequality. Sure Start Children's Centres – still a comparatively new service for 0 to 5 year olds have been established to help provide health and education services in the early years of a child's life alongside schools, community health services and GP practices. At the time of writing there are almost 3,000 Sure Start Children's Centres open, and by 2010 there will be 3,500 – that is one in every local community. Schools too, increasingly see children's health and well-being as central to their role. The majority of schools have now achieved Healthy Schools and Extended School status (with over 60% of schools in both programmes). This translates to around 3.7 million children are currently attending a Healthy School and say they feel healthier, happier and safer, while parents say they feel more involved in the children's health and learning. A 'healthy' picture indeed.

The development of health and bodily awareness

Policy changes in public health in recent years have seen a shift away from protecting from illness and disease to a new focus on individual behaviour and lifestyle risk factors and the broader determinants of health, like poverty and education (Wanless, 2004). In 2004 the launch of *Every Child Matters: Change for Children* (DfES, 2004) put health firmly in the public spotlight. The aims in this powerful document were, for every child whatever their background or circumstances, to have the support they need and were set out under the now familiar five ECM outcomes: to be healthy; to stay safe; to enjoy and achieve; to make a positive contribution and to achieve economic well-being. A particular focus of Every Child Matters to deliver the outcome for children to be healthy was on more integrated support through the delivery of services around the needs of children and families. The same message about integrating services to improve health outcomes came across strongly in the Government's White Paper *Choosing Health: Making Healthier Choices Easier* (DH, 2004a) in the same year, and offered practical advice about making informed choices and adopting a healthier lifestyle. The National Service Framework for Children, Young People and Maternity Services put in place for the first time national standards for children's health and social care (DH/DfES, 2004). It aimed, together with a new Child Health Promotion Programme for children from pre-birth through too adulthood, to promote physical and mental health and emotional well-being. The Common Assessment Framework (CAF) aimed at identifying and intervening to help children with additional needs to help them progress to the five Every Child Matters outcomes. It contains a checklist to help practitioners identify children who would benefit from a common assessment and asks if the child is healthy, safe from harm, learning and developing, has a positive impact on others and free from the negative influence of poverty. The National Occupational Standards in Children's Care, Learning and Development are standards for those who work with children aged 0–16 and specify the skills, knowledge and understanding required to do so effectively. The standards cover a wide range of settings including crèches, childminder's homes, Nurseries, playgroups, children's centres, extended schools, hospitals and SureStart programmes. Relevant units accredited at Level 3 include promoting children's well-being and resilience and developing and maintain a healthy, safe and secure environment for children.

There are objectives in the Children's Plan (DCSF, 2007) relating to securing the health and well-being of children and safeguarding the young and vulnerable. The Government's notion of a 'healthy child' is visible in the recently published *Next Steps for Early Learning and Childcare* (DCSF, 2009a) in which it restates a commitment to support families who care for children with high levels of need such as children with disabilities. Children's health and well-being needs are increasingly being met by the increased range of services offered by Sure Start Children's Centres, which aim to provide integrated health and family support services to support the whole family's needs. By 2010, all children should have access to the core offer of extended services in and around schools. In schools, *healthy eating*, personal, social and health education, *physical activity* and *emotional well-being* are core themes of the National Healthy Schools Programme This programme is designed to equip children with the skills and knowledge to make informed health and life choices and to reach their full potential. Evidence from an Ofsted in 2006a survey of 18 schools showed that the majority of schools in the survey were making a valuable contribution to pupils' health and well-being. The inspectors reported that some of the schools had redesigned their school improvement plans so that the framework of the Every Child Matters agenda guided many of their actions. Schools saw their responsibilities not only as teaching children about safety and healthy living, but also helping them to adopt healthier lifestyles, enhance their self-esteem, and eat and drink wisely. The Department of Health's *Healthy weight, Healthy lives: A cross-government strategy for England* (DH/DoH, 2008) was the next step in achieving the ambition of maintaining a healthy weight for everyone. It was also the Government's response to the influential Foresight report (2007) which gave the alarming message that nearly 60%of the UK population is on a trajectory to becoming obese by 2050; or putting this another way means that almost 2/3 of the population is classed as severely overweight. By 2020 the aim is to reduce the proportion of overweight and obese children to 2000 levels (Foresight report, 2007: v). The strategy describes the implications of this for schools and importantly has an initial and welcome focus on children.

The effects of environmental hazards upon children's health were reviewed through the publication of the Children's Environment and Health Strategy (HPA, 2009) which recognized the benefits of a clean and healthy environment and reported that the UK is in a relatively good position regarding environmental health. The document stresses that children and young people are especially vulnerable to environmental determinants of disease because are still growing and developing and their biological systems are more susceptible to harm from environmental hazards than adults, and immunity to disease is not as well developed; they often experience different patterns and levels of exposure to environmental hazards than adults because they take in more food, water and air per kilogram body weight than adults, they consume a different diet, they can absorb some chemicals more readily than adults and can be more vulnerable to unintentional injuries due to their tendency for exploratory behaviour, play and their relative inability to judge risks (HPA, 2009: 8). The Government's commitment in the Children's Plan to publish the first ever child health strategy came about with *Healthy lives, brighter futures: The strategy for children and young people's health* (DCSF, 2009b) and highlighted the Government's commitment to improving children's health. Published on 12 February 2009, this £372 million cross-government strategy presents the Government's vision for children and young people's health and well-being and supports the creation of a healthy society and includes early years, schools and food, sport and physical activity, transport and the health service. There is a focus in the Strategy on engaging the whole family in promoting child's health and well-being in five key areas: healthy growth and development of children identifies at risk families as early as possible and promote breastfeeding for mothers; promoting healthier food choices support parents in making changes to their children's diet and levels of physical activity; building physical activity into our lives reviews our nation's approach to physical activity and includes the role of Sport England, so there is a clear legacy of increased physical activity leading up to and after the 2012 Games; creating incentives for better health and finally giving personalized advice and support on diet and activity levels clearly and consistently. A cross-government initiative announced in July 2008 was that offering free swimming for the under 16s' and £25 million per annum in 2009–2010 and 2010–2011 being made available and £10 million in capital funding in to modernize swimming pool provision. Policies on active travel focus predominantly on journeys to and from schools, aiming to increase the number of children who walk and cycle regularly. Initiatives to make streets more attractive to pedestrians and cyclists and reduce traffic speed parking areas and redesigning play areas and open spaces to facilitate play for children and young people are evident. In order to achieve better health, increased physical activity and decreases in overweight and obesity figures, are a challenging set of national and local targets. The three-year Public Service Agreements (PSAs) include targets to reduce child poverty (PSA 9), improve the health and well-being of children and young people (PSA 12), improve child safety (PSA 13), increase the number of children and young people on the path to success (PSA 14), provide better health and better care for all, including tackling health inequalities (PSAs 18 and 19), and deliver a sustainable Olympic legacy with more children and young people participating in physical education and sport (PSA 22).

The messages about good physical and mental health are very clear in the Early Years Foundation Stage. The Welfare requirements tell us that children learn best when they are healthy, safe and secure, when their individual needs are met and when they have positive relationships with adults caring for them (EYFS, Practice Guidance, 2008: 14). Health has particular relevance to the guiding themes and principles underpinning effective practice in the EYFS. It also makes clear how health and well-being relate to the areas of Learning and Development. In Personal, Social and Emotional Development, opportunities for sharing thinking, to have conversations with others, to play alone and in pairs or groups promotes confidence and helps children feel good about themselves. Knowledge about health and well-being can be extended through activities in Communication, Language and Literacy in the home-corner, hospital play, with Small world and dolls' houses. Discussions at meal times, during food preparation and in outdoor activities are natural sources for quality conversation with children. Food and physical activity are two crucial areas in Problem-Solving, Reasoning and Numeracy. Knowledge and Understanding of the World can stimulate children's curiosity and extend knowledge about foods, farming and cooking, the environment, the local neighbourhood and the people and cultures with whom they share their worlds. Young children draw on their experiences and knowledge of Health and Well-being in their fantasy play, retelling of stories, using and making puppets, poetry, paintings, dance, music and other modes of the 'hundred languages of children' (Malaguzzi, 1993). It is centrally implicated in the Unique Child in Physical

Development, supporting understanding of how physical activities, food and drink, sleep, safety and hygiene are vital to life as we shall explore in this chapter. Figure 2.2 illustrates the key messages The Early Years Foundation Stage (Effective Practice: Health and Well-being, 2007).

- Resilience is promoted through attachment and each child being special to at least one significant person.
- Children's dietary and physical needs underpin their ability to develop.
- Opportunities to explore and play in a safe and secure environment, and children's mobility and movement, are important for their development.
- Brain development depends on nourishment: a good diet, in both the form of food and of physical and psychological stimulation.
- Reasonable rules, which fit with children's rhythms and give a pattern to life, matter.
- Parents, as well as children, need support.
- Young children enjoy contributing to life in their setting and being with their friends.
- Child abuse, neglect and failure to thrive impact on children's Health and Well-being.
- Babies and young children with special needs have additional requirements. They need access to similar experiences and opportunities as other children, in both a philosophical as well as practical sense.
- It is important that each child knows their key person.
- Senior practitioners in your setting should be designated and trained to be responsible for child protection issues and health and safety.
- Communities and the public need help to understand the importance of positive interactions and experiences in the first five years of life, for all areas of development and for enjoyment in the here and now.
- Strong links between the setting and other professionals such as health visitors and community paediatricians are vital.

Figure 2.2 EYFS Effective Practice: Health and Well-being messages

Support for health and bodily awareness

In their review of the research evidence on early interventions to enhance the health of children and their families, Barnes and Freude-Lagevardi (2002)

indicate that both professionals and para-professionals, working alongside families, should share decision making and that both pre- and post-natal interventions, which do not try to operate on too many fronts at the same time, are likely to prove most effective. Children's health and well-being needs are increasingly being met by the increased range of services offered by Sure Start Children's Centres, which aim to provide integrated health and family support services to support the whole family's needs. Many Children Centres provide help and advice with breastfeeding, through sessions run by volunteers. Sessions offered include Baby Massage classes, Yoga or consultations with the Health Visitor provide much needed practical support to parents. Not forgetting dads, too. There are many programmes specifically to include and up-skill dads as parents. One such centre we visited has recently opened a café which serves healthy breakfast and lunches, successfully spreading the message of healthy eating in one local community. New qualifications, standards and assessments are emerging that map to *Every Child Matters* and aim to ensure that every child is healthy, safe from harm, learning and developing. These identify the need for a language common language across agencies that include health, education and all aspects of care and development and across the range of early years settings and importantly, the need for agencies to work together to promote children's health.

Health and bodily awareness from birth to 3 years of age

Establishing activity from an early age makes a vital contribution to young children's healthy development. Activity for children begins in the womb. Much movement takes place in utero, as many mothers will remember the kicking, wriggling and frequent changing of position especially in the later stages of pregnancy. Through such movements information is given to the foetus about the surroundings and allows exploration of that environment (Hannaford, 1995). It is also excellent exercise! Advances in new technology allows us to see foetal movements that include independent finger movements, thumb sucking, yawning, hand contact with the face and head rotation and flexion. Research by Campbell (2004) tells us that a foetus can run a hand constantly over the face, suck a fist, scratch and pat a cheek, brings both knees up, takes hold of the umbilical cord and use it as a pillow. From being born, babies are well equipped for survival and arrive in the world with a range of reflexes, capabilities and an appetite to find out and to move. The first 3 years are the important 'starting points' for a child's healthy journey' through life. Mellilo and Leisman (2004) tell us that movement is crucially important for the growing child and that the human brain was born out of movement. Babies' first language is indeed movement and what was once considered as random flailing of arms and legs we now recognize as a way for them to do exactly this: signal their needs, discover their new world and communicate with others. Hodgson makes this point in informing us that 'everything that we discover about life, we discover through movement' (2001: 172). They delight in these early movements and it is here that foundations for continued movement experiences begin and the satisfaction that this brings with it.

What also characterises new babies' activity is how organized they are in their daily patterns. Over a 24-hour cycle, newborns show six different states of consciousness ranging from varying degrees of sleep, crying, to alert activity phases. In these phases are short bursts of movement of the types described earlier. These often appear as intense motions of arms and legs, separately and together that are often accompanied by burbles of delight. Quite right. Moving is fun! By recognizing the different states and realizing when these take place, parents and professionals can assess the general health of a baby and identify if any developmental problems are emerging. Confining babies and young children to strollers, play pens and car seats for long periods can cause development delays physically as well as cognitive. By far the best way to encourage movement is through play. Play allows babies and toddlers to learn about themselves and the world that surrounds them. They do not separate play times from learning or other times. Their play *is* their learning and vice versa. Bruce writes of play as a 'learning mechanism' (2005: 131) and one that fulfils a supporting role by helping children under-three to develop their bodies, find out about safety and make healthy choices as part of living and learning. It helps them become competent learners who are able to make connections, be imaginative, creative and represent their experiences. Play also provides an excellent medium for healthy exercise.

In these formative years, self-initiated play should dominate physical activity to develop early motor skills and provide health benefits relating to weight management.

Photograph 2.2 Physically active play

Physically active play defined by Livingstone and colleagues as, 'all locomotor physical activity, which involves large muscle groups to move the body
around and to apply force to objects' (Livingstone, 2003: 682). This type of
activity is the first and most frequent expression of play in infancy (Bailey,
1999). Active play supports children's physical development, intellectual capacity, builds self-confidence, communication skills and it helps them form relationships with others. On the floor they change from lying on tummies to
being on their front. When they are strong enough they can stretch up and
arch their backs with amazingly supple spines and push off from straight arms
to hold their necks up. What a new vista that opens up for them. The pushing
and pulling and sliding movements relay vital information about themselves
in space and the floor or other surface in which they move and is the foundation of proprioception, the sense that provides information on the body's
actions. Other physical activity include supporting body weight through rocking and rolling. Crawling on tummies is the first self-determined locomotor
action and leads onto crawling which is a motor skill with a powerful combi-
nation of balance and travel and probably equates to driving a car for the first
time in its sense of mastery and enjoyment. Horizontal locomotor movement

actions easily observed in the under 3s' include crawling (at 6 months on average) creeping (at 9 months on average) through to achievement of upright gait and independent walking (between 10 and 15 months) and a baby's first steps and progress to the 'furniture walkabout' (Davies, 2003: 45) – a lovely way of describing a toddlers journey from one place to another with help from strategically placed pieces of furniture to assist. Spinning, tipping, tilting, falling help build the vestibular sense, that of balance and sense of space (Greenland, 2006). Handling objects is important too. A baby's grip and release of a toy are precursors of later throwing and catching actions.

Aquatic environments are places in which babies feel very much at home and water activity brings many health benefits. Bath times at home are the best way for a baby to experience the gentleness and soothing of water and recall the 9 months spent suspended in the amniotic fluid of the womb. Bath times are times of enjoyment for a baby and provide a natural place to exercise arms and legs, enjoy the sensation of floating and be introduced to early buoyancy. Water is a great activity to improve posture. When the child is ready the transition to a small well-heated indoor pool extends this further and provides a wonderful opportunity for bonding with a new child. Progression from the early swimming (amphibian) reflex to conscious 'swimming type' actions at around 6 months build confidence, engenders feelings of happiness and security, enables communication between parent and child and provide true health benefits for the child. Eye contact between adult and child is promoted coordination is improved in this multi-sensory environment. Since there is no gravity, a much greater range of movements are possible without the restrictions that being unable to sit upright or stand have and a greater range of muscle are exercised. The emphasis with babies is on having fun as they discover about buoyancy in a playful relaxed atmosphere and develop strength as they wriggle and kick. Some favourite water activities for parents and carers include:

- Supporting the baby's back and let the infant experience assisted floating
- Parent back floats and gently propels with baby held on tummy or on chest
- Holding the baby facing the water, place a toy or bright object in front to encourage arm movements and head lifting
- Perform the seat hold – one hand around the baby's waist and the other supporting the seat, walk the baby through the water
- Blowing bubbles to encourage exhaling

- Launching out from the side to meet another parent and baby in the water
- Holding the infant's extended hands and arms while the child is supine to help body alignment.

As the child's confidence and proficiency grows, time in the pool can be extended and other games can be added with equipment such as woggles to add extra support, balls to bat around, arm bands etc. to increase their range of movement and provide increased exercise. Maude (2001) reports that 3-year-old children have the highest activity levels of any age in the human life-span. They are constantly in motion and to satisfy this need demands daily exercise and opportunities for them to be active. Just how active are young children is explored in more depth in the case study that follows.

Photograph 2.3 Chopping tomatoes (photograph by Lindy Nahmad-Williams)

Case study

The recent publication *Play and Exercise in Early Years: Physically active play in early childhood provision* (Brady et al., 2008) focused on the extent to which children

Case study—Cont'd

were involved in physically active play. The researchers defined physically active play as 'any physical activity where the child is doing what they want to do for their own reasons' (p. 6) and distinguished this play from more structured activity where children are being 'instructed', or play that involved little physical activity. Their investigation involved observations of children's activity in 19 different settings and semi-structured interviews with parents and setting staff. This enabled a detailed record of children's activity in relation to the environment and interactions with adults to be built up. Part of the sample involved children under-three who were independently mobile (i.e. at the crawling stage and older), mixed by gender and ethnicity.

Key findings relevant to the under-threes were:

- There was substantial variation in activity levels between children.
- Activity levels were patterned neither by gender nor age, with the exception that two 11-month olds were by some way the least active.
- The proportion of observed time children spent in physically active play varied between settings.
- On average each child was involved in 2.7 types of physically active play per observation – or 1.9 types other than walking, which was the most frequently noted activity.
- An average of 8 minutes in every 15 minute observation period included some physically active play, with variations between settings and children.
- The physical layout of the settings had a substantial impact on both the type of play children engaged in and how active children were.
- It was rare for children not to be physically active when they were outside, and some more vigorous activities occurred more frequently outside than inside.

The study concluded that physically active play in early years is influenced by a range of factors that included the ethos of the setting and support and encouragement from staff at an individual child level. Other factors impacting on the quality and the quantity of play reported included the layout and design of the setting, opportunities for self-directed activity, (free) access to outside space, and equipment and activities that were suitable for the age group. Age, nature and other characteristics of the individual child had an impact on how active a child was and the type of activities they engaged in.

Reflection for early career professional

- What activities in a setting would promote daily physical activity in the youngest children?
- How would this differ for a baby of 10 months and a young child of 30 months?
- How would this be different indoors and outside?

Reflection for leader/manager

- Consider how you would ensure that all setting staff understand that babies and young children need adequate time and resources for them to be physically active and promote this in their practice?

Early movement is also how babies communicate their feelings and needs. It is also part of their emotional well-being. Because their language is as yet limited, facial expressions, body language and gestures become important ways for adults to understand the emotional needs of the under-threes. The relationship between emotional health and other aspects of a child's development are obvious, but to Trisha David, they are even more wide reaching. She believes 'emotional well-being is the bedrock on which all later development depends' (David, 2004: 21). *Birth to Three Matters* (DfES, 2002) made a number of important points in summarizing children's emotional well-being that are worth reminding ourselves of at this point: Young babies are primed to become social beings. Warm, mutual, affirmative relationships give babies the courage to express their feelings. They crave close attachments with a special person and when they have a close relationship with a warm and responsive adult, they explore from a safe place to which they can return. As children learn to do things for themselves they gain confidence, knowing that the adult is close by, ready to support and help if needed.

Good nutrition is also crucial for good mental and physical health. The report *Food and nutrition for the under-threes: A discussion document* (Infant and Toddler Forum, 2009 looked at the importance of diet for the under-threes and gives the results of a survey of 1,000 parents in which it found that

- Nearly a third of the respondents' under-threes eat at least one take-away meal a week
- Nineteen per cent are given take-aways and ready meals every day
- Sixty-five per cent of mothers never cook meals from scratch for their toddlers
- Twenty-nine per cent of under-threes have chocolate and sweets almost every day
- Sixteen per cent have fizzy drinks almost every day
- Ninety-five per cent were following Government guidelines to feed their toddler like the rest of the family.

Alarming figures indeed. Nutrition for good health begins in the prenatal period with a diet that supplies correct nutrients for brain and body development. The developing foetus requires proper nutrients for growth simply because it is totally reliant upon the mother to provide this. The need for proper nutrition continues its importance through the early years of life. Proper nutrition is the body's first line of defence against illness and being well nourished positively affects how children learn and think. Studies have found a link between low birthweight and health status in later life. Babies who are underweight at birth but who 'catch up' within the first 2–3 years of infancy have increased risk of disease as adults (Barker et al., 2001). The lack of muscle at birth is compensated by an increase in body weight which in turn can lead to levels of fat causing diabetes and heart disease. Breast-feeding is generally agreed to be the optimum method for feeding babies since it provides all the energy, liquid and nutrients in the form of essential *protein*, and *carbohydrate* and fats for growth and development. Breast-feeding benefits both mother and baby. It strengthens the immune system, builds bone density, assists with absorption of iron and can help the mother regulate excess weight gain (Akobeng et al., 2006). It should also continue beyond 6 months as an accompaniment to appropriate weaning foods. Breastfeeding has also been found to have a small but consistent effect on childhood obesity (Arenz et al., 2004). On average, 100 grams of human milk provides 289 kJ (69 kcal) of energy, 1.3 g protein, 4.1 g fat, 7.2 g carbohydrate (mainly lactose) and 34 mg calcium and during the first 3 months, mothers of fully breast-fed babies produce about 800 ml of milk a day. This amount is consistent for women all over the world (see British Nutrition Foundation, 2009). Apart from the nutritional benefits of breastfeeding, the positive stimulation it provides to babies is important in forming close attachments between mother and baby and has been found to positively influence brain development (McCain and Mustard, 1999). For mothers who cannot or choose not to breast-feed, formula milk is recommended, which has a composition of protein, fat and carbohydrate similar to human milk. The Infant Feeding Survey 2005 (Bolling et al., 2007) reveals that the percentage of babies still being exclusively breastfed at 6 months is less than 1 per cent. And breastfeeding rates in the United Kingdom are the lowest in Europe. In response, a National Helpline for Breastfeeding Mothers was launched in February 2008, providing practical support and advice to 450,000 breastfeeding mothers in England. A breastfeeding campaign was launched in May 2008, to encourage young mothers from low-income backgrounds to breastfeed for longer. Sharon, a mother of 3-year-old Kelly had attended the sessions at her local Children's Centre had this to say, 'the sessions are great and have really helped me. Kelly was born premature and had no sucking action. With help from the group we overcame this and I managed to breastfeed her for about three months.' Advice and support from experienced professionals helped this young mum.

Health and bodily awareness from 3 to 5 years of age

In the period from 3 to 5 years, children become increasingly more active. Developing motor skills and greater mobility allow them to explore further afield. They are curious to discover what the exciting world offers them. They love to be active and delight in trying out new physical skills, practising established ones and testing their limits in ingenious ways (Doherty and Bailey, 2003). There have been many myths over the years about how much exercise children need and since the 1990s a recognition that what is suitable for adults (both in type of exercise and duration), is not appropriate to children gaining optimal health. It is worth stating that activities for this age group should resemble natural physical play as much as possible. This is the time to practise and refine gross motor skills by running, jumping and climbing trees or apparatus and to use the outdoor environment as much as possible. Many Nurseries encourage children to use tools in gardening. Heart fitness is increased by walking to and back from nursery, using bikes and trikes, chasing games, rough and tumble play and playground games. Traditional street games like Grandma's Footsteps, What time is it, Mr Wolf?, Hide and Seek and Hopscotch are certain to raise the pulse. Many outdoor areas have ground markings painted on them which allow a great many active games or a large activity circuit where children move between the markings running, hopping and jumping. Rope-skipping is an excellent aerobic activity that is also a difficult skill to master. Parachute games are to be recommended and can be used with large groups of Nursery and Reception age children with adult support. Here are some examples. *Statues* – 3 children go under the chute and form a statue while the rest of the group try to make a high mushroom shape overhead with the chute. *Ripples* – a large group stand around the parachute and move their wrists and arms in small motions to send ripples around the outside. Experiment with different speeds. *Up to the Top, Down to the Bottom* – a large group stand around the parachute and move their arms with large movements to raise the chute above head height and then down again to below knee height. *Popcorn* – a group of children stand around the chute. A light ball is placed in the centre and the challenge is to make the ball bounce while keeping it on the chute.

Photograph 2.4 Early Swimming (© P. Hopkins)

Experimenting with small equipment such as bats and balls develop gross and fine motor skills through such activities as

- throwing beanbags to targets
- bouncing balls on the spot and then moving
- rolling quoits along the ground
- rolling a hoop to a partner
- throwing balls – 2 handed
- throwing a small ball – 1 handed
- kicking a ball for distance
- dribbling a ball around cones
- balancing a small ball on top of a flat bat
- striking a ball with a bat
- catching balls at different heights.

Many familiar chasing games are first-rate stamina builders – tag games, tag games where the tagger is only allowed to tag only a particular body part, tag games with more than one chaser, Catch my Tail, Octopus, etc. These are catching games. Catch My Tail is a game where one child has a braid or band tucked into the top of their trousers or skirt at the back with most of it hanging out. Other children try to capture that tail as the child with the tail tries to avoid cit being captured. It is great fun with a small group and with other children as a partner game. Octopus is a running and chasing game where children run past the 'octopus', who tries to catch them. (The octopus' stays in a designated area that the children must run past.) Anyone caught becomes a tentacle on the octopus helping to catch too and the game continues until all the other children are caught .Children of this age benefit enormously from body management activities. Travelling on feet, or with feet and hands together, animal walks (Walk like a bear, like a rabbit, like a kangaroo) are extremely energetic. Movements where children support their body weight like hanging from apparatus, supporting themselves on hands and feet and transferring weight through rolling and jumping are to be encouraged. Moving to taped music and responding to different types of music or simple percussion through movement help children understand about their bodies in space and help them communicate their feelings in a physical way. Tumble Tot classes, yoga, Gymtots and classes to develop ball skills are to be found in every locality.

Many 'fitness' activities easily lend themselves to be shared with parents at home. Here are a few ideas

- Bicycles – lying on backs with raised legs, soles of feet against each other and perform a bicycle action in a continuous motion;
- Row the boat – face each other seated on the floor with soles against each other. Take hold of each other's outstretched hands and row back and forward together;
- Horsey – the adult sits on a chair with the child on her knees, held firmly. The adult bounces the child first as a trot, then faster to a canter and even a gallop;
- Bottom shuffle – a race shuffling on bottoms;
- Ball pass – this time sit facing each other and pass the ball to each other by extended legs;
- Balance time – who can balance on one leg for longest. Who can balance on 2 feet and 1 hand for longest?
- Shall we jump? Holding hands and facing each other, jump together in rhythm ten times.

The best form of physical activity should be enjoyable; it must appeal to children and be as natural and as normal to their everyday life as possible (Doherty and Bailey, 2003). New guidelines (NICE, 2009) have been recently published, providing guidance on promoting physical activity, active play and sport for children in family, pre-school, school and community settings. Play England contributed to the guidelines and Issy Cole-Hamilton, Head of Policy and Research said: 'With fewer places where children feel safe to play outside, and ever increasing traffic in residential areas, today's children are becoming less and less active. By providing children and young people with spaces and staffed facilities where they feel safe to play freely with their friends, we are giving them the chance to be more physically active while enjoying the sense of freedom that this offers them.' Current guidelines recommend that children and young people should do a minimum of 60 minutes of at least moderate-intensity physical activity each day. At least twice a week, this should include activities to improve bone health (weight-bearing activities that produce high physical stresses on the bones, such as running and jumping), muscle strength and flexibility (DH, 2004b). Activities need to vary in intensity. This age group do not move continuously for extended periods of time as adults can. Their activity patterns show spontaneous and intermittent bouts: stopping and starting, short durations lasting several seconds are common.

They need regular low, moderate and sometimes vigorous intensities with frequent rest periods as needed on an individual basis accumulating up to 60 minutes of moderate activity each day. (Moderate-intensity activity increases breathing and heart rates to a level where the pulse can be felt and the child feels warmer. Vigorous activity results in being out of breath or sweating). Children in the 3–5 age range need a place to play, things to play with and time to play.

Attachment is the emotional bond young children develop with (significantly) their parents (and the mother in particular although by no means exclusively) in their earliest years. Many children from 3–5 are cared for by adults other than their parents. While time spent in various settings varies considerably, the critical factor is the quality of the experiences received during this time. The EYFS champions the role of the key person and makes it mandatory for each child in a Nursery setting or Reception class to be allocated a key person. This is a named member of staff who has more contact than others with a particular child, who builds relationships with the child and parents, is 'tuned in' and able to meet the child's individual needs and responds sensitively to feelings and behaviour. This is an important role across the EYFS and 'settling in' to a new setting, saying good byes in the morning, daily care routines like toileting, getting changed, eating, resting or sleeping can have an important and lasting effect on a child's emotional health. As professionals we need to understand a child's needs and the impact that important events like transitions can have on children and parents. There are likely to be many transitions in a child's life. For this age group transitions might include from room to room in the same setting; from home to a setting; from one setting to another or into school. These can be exciting times but not to be underestimated in the effect they can have on the child.

Reflective task

Making transitions a positive experience requires time and planning and an understanding the impact that 'settling in' can have on a child and the family. It requires a flexible approach so that individual emotional needs are met and information shared about the child's likes, dislikes, interests and experiences and health status

⇨

Reflective task—Cont'd

between the setting and the child's parents. Conversations with parents and setting staff on 'settling in' echo this:

Parent: 'The staff at the Nursery asked me lots of questions. I felt they took a lot of time to get to know Cheryl. I thought this was good and felt that they wanted to know a lot about Cheryl before she arrived. It really did help her settle in.'

Nursery Practitioner: ' We use a lot of photographs with parents. They like to see what their child has been doing during the day with us. I think it helps to reassure them and they feel their child is happy with us'.

Parent: 'I was anxious about Tamsin starting a new Nursery. The staff were great. It helped talking through things with them. I felt I wanted to tell them everything! She is so happy there and so much more confident now'.

Nursery Manager: 'Its about team working. That's what makes the difference. Everyone knows what is expected and we all want the same for every child in the Nursery'.

Reflection for early career professional

- What practical ways can practitioners ensure that all transitions meet the individual needs and interests of each child? In what ways can parents be involved – before, during and afterwards?

Reflection for leader/manager

- How can leaders and managers influence smooth transitions? Are there staff training needs to be addressed, for example, knowledge of child development or practice issues, for example, transition planning and procedures?

Good nutrition is also important for good health. During the time of rapid growth from 3 to 5 years, children need high energy foods that are also rich in nutrients and eaten as part of 'little' and 'often' meals. The British Nutrition Foundation advises that children of this age require a good supply of protein, calcium, iron and vitamins A and D. Calcium is important for healthy tooth development and with vitamin D, helps strengthen growing bones. The Foundation recommends that children are taught to think about dental hygiene and encouraged to reduce the number of times a day that they have foods and have sugary drinks and, if possible, to have them only at meal times. Regular teeth brushing with a fluoride toothpaste and regular visits to the dentist is also encouraged. In excess of 600,000 children in England and Wales attend Nurseries and some of these children the time can spend be up to 10 hours a day in settings. Naturally parents expect a safe environment and a nurturing environment and the food their children eat there to be subject to and meet regulatory and nutritional guidelines. In many cases, Nurseries provide most of the daily food since children will eat some food during the day, and a significant minority of children who attend Nursery 'full time' will be eating the majority of their food in Nurseries. Just what is the picture about healthy eating for this age group?

From 2003 to 2005, Ofsted carried out a programme of inspections against the ECM standards which included healthy eating (Ofsted, 2005). They found that half the 94,000 registered settings provided good quality childcare by meeting national standards well and often exceeding them. Children learned about healthy eating and had a balanced diet. Good providers promoted children's health by taking a range of positive actions to encourage healthy eating and prevent obesity. Children were helped to enjoy food and understand why some foods are healthy and others are not. They helped prepare meals and snacks. Mealtimes were relaxed, social occasions when children and adults sat together around the table to enjoy their food and each other's company. Staff were aware of the many learning opportunities to promote an understanding of healthy eating. In good settings children's health was promoted by a wholesome, nutritious and balanced diet. Meals were freshly prepared using fresh fruit and vegetables, some using organic and even home-grown produce. Processed food was not served and children are not given food and drinks with high levels of artificial additives and sugar. Menus were produced to give parents information about meal choices. They included dishes from different cultures. Drinking water was always available. Providers were aware of each child's individual dietary needs and ensured these were met. In 2006 a short survey presented a positive picture of the quality of food given to children in registered childcare (Ofsted, 2006b). The majority of practitioners visited in this survey had a good knowledge of healthy eating, provided a nutritious and balanced diet for young children in their care and promoted healthy eating to parents and children.

The picture is far from good with reports of Nurseries spending as little as 25p per child on food each day. It appears that some Nurseries were applying the principles of adult healthy eating to the food they were supplying to young children, putting them at risk of developing nutritional deficiencies. A damning report published by the Soil Association entitled *Georgie Porgie Pudding and Pie Exposing the truth about nursery food* (Soil Association, 2008) went further. This was the first detailed investigation into the state of food for young children attending Nurseries in England and Wales and presented some alarming findings

- Some Nurseries regularly serve food that includes crisps, chocolate, lollies, sweets, cakes, biscuits, burgers and chips.
- Nurseries are serving food to children under the age of three that contain additives.
- Many children in Nurseries are consuming food high is fat, sugar and salt.
- How well a child will be fed at nursery, and how well its health is.
- Protected, relies on where they live, whether the nursery is committed to good food and what parents can afford.
- Many parents and nursery staff are unhappy with the current 'unregulated' state of nursery food.
- There is no compulsory training for nursery staff serving food.
- There are no clear national nutritional standards.
- No agency monitors the quality of food provided.
- No Government funding is available to help Nurseries improve provision.

(A word of caution. The research also reported that many Nurseries provided an exceptional service to the children in their care and gave examples of high quality, freshly prepared, locally sourced sometimes organic food in all sectors of Nursery provision). In short says the research, 'Nursery food provision is letting children down' (p. 15). It argued that the legal requirements covering food in Nurseries are inferior to those in schools. This research presents a convincing case for change. There is currently no detailed legislation for meals provided in childcare settings. Ofsted guidelines (Ofsted, 2001) and the DfES publication Healthy School Lunches for Pupils in Nursery Schools/Units (2000) DFES (2000) remain vague and open to interpretation.

Has anything changed? Fortunately yes. Healthy Start, a government initiative to help families from low income and disadvantaged households in the UK, by giving vouchers for free milk and fresh fruit and vegetables to parents of young children and pregnant mothers is now more widely publicized. There have been changes outlining the changes in the nature and of food and drink advertising and promotion to children. The 5 A-Day scheme and the 5 A-Day School Fruit and Vegetable aim to increase fruit and vegetable consumption as a national priority. In January 2009 the Food Standards Agency began an advertising campaign to raise awareness of the health risks of eating too much saturated fat. The School Food Trust is an agency set up by Government to oversee implementation of the new statutory nutrient-based standards for school food. The Government has announced new standards for school food in all local authority maintained primary, secondary, special and boarding schools, and Pupil Referral Units in England. The new standards cover all food sold or served in schools (breakfast, lunch and after-school meals tuck, vending machines, mid-morning break and after-school clubs). Advice on nutrition appears on the Surestart website. The Food Standards Agency's website gives useful information on healthy eating including the Eatwell plate (an updated version of 'The Balance of Good Health' plate) and practical advice on what to put in children's lunch boxes. Following the Ofsted report *Starting early: Food and nutrition education of young children* in 2004, food policies are now seen as a crucial first step to ensuring a common approach for playgroups, Nurseries or schools and allow children, staff, governors, parents/carers, helpers or caterers to have a shared understanding of healthy eating. Many settings now provide policies and sample weekly menus on their home pages.

With due regard to individual needs and to cultural practices, by the time a child is five they should be eating a healthy diet based on the types and proportions of foods represented in the Eatwell plate and eating a variety of foods from the five main groups (for further information see The Caroline Walker Trust website (www.cwt.org.uk/publications.html).

(1) Bread, rice, potatoes, pasta and other starchy foods – this food group is an important source of energy and provides fibre, B Vitamins and iron. Children in this age group should be encouraged to eat. (2) A variety of fruit and vegetables to provide essential vitamins and minerals, particularly vitamin C, fibre and antioxidants. The good news is that this can be fresh,

frozen, dried or tinned and all counts as part of the 5 A-Day target. (3) Meat, Fish, eggs, beans and other non-dairy sources of protein are good sources of protein and also provide iron, zinc, magnesium and Vitamin B12. (4) The milk and diary food group is a good source of calcium, protein, fat, vitamin A and D. Vegetarians should eat eggs, milk, dairy and honey or meat alternatives like lentils, beans, chickpeas and meat substitutes (such as tofu and quorn). Snacks for this age group tend to be mostly biscuits and crisps and children should be encouraged to snack on healthy foods like yoghurt, fresh fruit, homemade popcorn and raw vegetables. (5) Tea and coffee as drinks should be avoided and replaced with water, milk and pure unsweetened fruit juices. Fizzy drinks or those with artificial sweeteners should be avoided as they can cause poor appetite and a failure to thrive. The Caroline Walker Trust is a registered charity that promotes better public health through good food argues that nutrient-based standards are the most effective way to improve menu planning and has produced an electronic tool (CHOMP) to allow menus to be put together easily. Such innovative practice provides the necessary support for Early Years providers and sends a message to policy makers of the need to translate advice into action and take nutrition for the under 5s' seriously.

Childhood obesity

The years from birth to five are recognized as a critical period for children's development and health and when patterns and behaviours associated with eating healthily and being active are formed. There is certainly a lack of awareness in relation to the pre-school population and we know that poor nutrition and low levels of activity are major causes of childhood obesity. Excess weight comes at a high price for children. Everyday actions like walking are difficult. Skipping and impact activities are out of the question. A number of children struggle with games. There are also psychological consequences as well as physical and increasing numbers of children are experiencing problems with low esteem, concerns about body image, depression, bullying and social exclusion (Doherty and Whiting, 2004). Obesity is now a global epidemic and the sad truth is, it often begins in childhood.

Case study

In England, obesity levels have tripled in the past 20 years. Fourteen per cent of 2–15 year olds are obese and 18 per cent are overweight. Obesity is responsible for around 9,000 deaths each year and carries with it a reduction in life expectancy of 9 years on average (NAO, 2001). Projections are that if nothing is done to halt this trend, 25 per cent of children will be obese by 2050 and 30 per cent overweight (Foresight, 2007). According to the UK National BMI percentiles classification, around three in ten boys and girls aged 2–15 are classed as either overweight or obese (31 per cent and 30 per cent respectively). Between 1995 and 2007 there were year on year fluctuations in children's obesity levels. For children aged between 2–15, obesity has risen from 11 per cent of boys and 12 per cent of girls in 1995 to 17 per cent of boys and 16 per cent of girls in 2007. In the European Union nations, 3 million children are obese and 14 million are now overweight. These numbers show a rising figure of 400,000 each year in overweight children and 85,000 for obese children.

Professor Mike Kelly, Public Health Excellence Centre Director says: 'Obesity rates in this country are rocketing and with the number of children not taking part in physical activity increasing, this problem can only get worse. Dealing with the long term consequences of obesity costs an estimated £2.5 billion each year, placing a huge strain on the health service. It's important that we let children play, and don't let society's aversion to risk stop young people from being physically active.' More recent birth cohort studies show a much higher prevalence of childhood obesity (Law et al., 2007). There are now reported cases of maturity-onset diabetes in child-hood, which a decade ago would have been unknown. Poorly nourished children, particularly those who are overweight or obese, can experience social and psycho-logical problems (Janssen et al., 2004). The trend of weight problems in children is a particular cause for concern because of evidence suggesting a 'conveyor-belt' effect in which weight problems in childhood can continue into adulthood. Some groups are more at risk than others of becoming overweight or obese. Those with learning disabilities have a higher rate of obesity (35 per cent) than the general population (22 per cent) (Kerr, 2004). Certain minority ethnic groups, and principally females from those groups, are have excess weight problems. Girls, particularly from lower social groups and in Asian families tend to be overweight. Males however, from some minority ethnic groups appear to have markedly lower obesity levels. The 2004 Health Survey for England showed Black African children appear to have the highest levels of obesity (32 per cent of boys and 28 per cent of girls), followed

⇨

Case study—Cont'd

by Black Caribbean children (27 per cent of boys and 21 per cent of girls) and Bangladeshi children (24 per cent of boys and 21 per cent of girls). Pakistani and Irish boys also appear to have high levels of obesity with an obesity prevalence of 21 per cent and 20 per cent respectively. Bangladeshi and Pakistani males and females reported the lowest levels of physical activity in the survey.

Reflection for early career professional

- How healthy are the food and drinks you provide to children in your setting?
- Are there groups of children who are leas active than others?
- If so, what can you do to counter this?

Reflection for leader/manager

- Given these and similar research findings, how can you ensure that children eat a healthy diet in the setting and there is due regard to cultural practices and individual preferences?
- Do you know how active children are? Have you information on *all* children?

Transition to Key Stage 1 (5 to 7 years of age)

The transition from EYFS to Key Stage 1 should be a gradual one, aiming for consistency and progression that maintains experiential and active learning and offers a curriculum that is relevant and interesting for every child. Children's emotional health continues to be supported predominately through Personal, Social and Emotional Development but also as we have stressed in this chapter, comes under the umbrella term of 'health'. Mental health with this age group involves how children relate to each other, make friends, feel special and secure about themselves and learn confidently. You may wish to try these activities:

Practical tasks

- Create time for children to talk about themselves, their family and community
- Let children discuss how to avoid harm and ways to keep themselves safe
- Model language and behaviour when children wish to join in a game with others but are unable to find how to so they can use these strategies
- Play turn-taking games with a group of children and use language such as, 'Whose turn is it now? Is it your turn . . . (child's name)?'
- Give children with English not their first language opportunities to express themselves in their home language.

As children move from the EYFS to Key Stage 1, the requirement for them to eat healthily continues. There is much anecdotal evidence to suggest that when children have a nutritionally balanced diet they concentrate in the classroom better and their behaviour improves. There is a research link between nutrition and school performance and evidence suggests that children's diet affects their ability to learn. In a presentation of their research Sorhaindo and Sabates (2006) reported that the following conditions were linked to poor nutrition among school age children:

- Developmental disorders, for example, dyslexia and dyspraxia
- Obesity
- Memory
- Concentration
- Intelligence
- Attention span
- Attention-Deficit-Hyperactivity Disorder
- Aggression
- Achievement.

Three important findings came from their research. Nutrition prior to school entry appeared to be the most important predictor of school attainment. They found that early junk food dietary pattern remained a risk factor to school attainment, even when factors such as gender, ethnicity, mother's education, family, health and eating habits, parenting and income were taken into account. Thirdly, that the early consumption of junk food was also associated with attainment growth from entry to KS1 and from Key Stage 1 to Key Stage 2. Clear messages about the importance of healthy eating in the early childhood years.

Ideally, children going to school should do so after a full breakfast. Breakfast, is the first and some say, the most important meal of the day. For those children who for various reasons this is not possible, breakfast clubs offer well balanced food and a healthy start to the day. Children who have not had breakfast are more likely to suffer from poor memory and limited attention span and process information less effectively (Simeon and Grantham-McGregor, 1989). Findings of a study reported by the School Food Trust Eat Better Do Better (2008) in deprived areas of London 1 year after introducing breakfast clubs compared the results of a comparable group of schools without breakfast clubs and found their KS 2 results were significantly improved. The School Food Trust has been conducting research in the area of child nutrition and health, with a focus on school meals and examining if children eat better, do they do better. Evidence focusing on the nutrition and health of school-aged children in the United Kingdom, particularly focusing on school meals appears to be limited. Case studies and best practice guidance support improving nutrition at school to support children's behaviour, well-being and learning and there are numerous anecdotes from teachers and parents describing dramatic improvements in children's concentration, behaviour and academic performance when healthier school food is introduced. Yet no firm inferences can be drawn on the relationship between nutrition, including school food, and educational outcomes due to a lack of clear evidence. Nevertheless, schools remain important settings for children to learn about and put into practice good dietary habits. School health programmes can help children attain their full educational and health potential by providing them with the skills and social support they require to learn the basic fundamentals and importance of a healthy diet (Wood and Harper, 2008).

The broad base provided by the EYFS and its holistic nature should provide an effective platform for extending children's health knowledge and behaviours into the Primary School and National Curriculum Physical Education Programmes of Study at Key Stage 1 and beyond. Including all children in lifelong physical activity, sport and healthy lifestyles is not only desirable, it is the *only* possible course of action. It should be a 'planned-for lifelong process' that children seek out, that engages them in fun and relevant activities connected to experiences across the life-span. (Pickup, 2008: 82). Physical education and health have always been linked. Being physically active is part of a healthy lifestyle and PE should teach the necessary skills and understanding to encourage children to be active and to appreciate its benefits (Harris, 2000). A quality PE programme in Key Stage 1 should build upon the foundations in the EYFS and promote physical activity and healthy lifestyles and ensure safe practice. Programmes include knowledge, understanding, skills, attitudes and confidence with health-enhancing physical activity. Such programmes should encourage children to recognize, describe and understand the changes to their bodies during exercise and how these relate to good physical and mental health. Suggested content and expectations for health programmes for 5–7 year olds are shown in the Figure 2.3.

What 5–7 year olds should be able to know/do/understand about health		
Safety& Hygiene:	*Health:*	*Physical Activity:*
• know that a warm up before exercise is required • know that a cool down after exercise is required • appreciate that certain activities require appropriate clothing • have respect for equipment • adhere to simple safety rules • adhere to routines about personal hygiene	• know that physical activity improves health • know that physical activity & healthy eating help maintain a healthy weight • make informed choices about healthy food and drinks • appreciate that being healthy includes feeling good about oneself	• appreciate the importance of good posture • experience • changes to their bodies with exercise • be able to describe short-term changes to their bodies with exercise e.g. breathing faster; heart beat is faster; face flushed; muscles are worked; feelings of tiredness. • enjoy how it feels to be physically active • use opportunities to be regularly active in and out of school

(Continued)

What 5–7 year olds should be able to know/do/understand about health		
Strength activities	*Stamina activities*	*Flexibility activities*
<ul><li>Hops around mats</li><li>Jumps on/off benches</li><li>Jumps in/out of hoops</li><li>Balancing on one leg for 10 seconds</li><li>Shoulder circling</li><li>Seated. Practice swimming actions</li><li>Take weight on hands, lift leg to rear</li><li>Body weight on hands and feet in extended position for 5 seconds</li><li>Lying on back on the floor. Lift legs and cycle in the air</li><li>Lying on back. Alternate holding relaxed whole body shape with tense shape ("Floppy spaghetti")</li><li>Jack in the box-jumps from crouch</li></ul>	<ul><li>Running at different speeds</li><li>Sprinting on the spot, then half speed, then low speed</li><li>Galloping</li><li>Bounding on two feet</li><li>Hopping</li><li>Rope skipping</li><li>Skipping to percussion beat</li><li>Zig-zag running</li><li>Chasing games</li><li>Traditional games</li><li>Follow-my-leader</li><li>Marching (Accompaniment Grand Old Duke of York)</li><li>Dancing</li><li>Sending and receiving a ball with a partner</li></ul>	<ul><li>Stretch tall</li><li>Stretch out wide</li><li>Curling up in a ball</li><li>Repeat stretches on the floor</li><li>Shaking body parts to music</li><li>Moving like a robot then like a rag doll</li><li>Windmills – with arms stretched above head bend from the waist</li><li>Yoga position cross legged. Bend to each side.</li><li>Cobra stretch. Lie on front with weight on hands, Raise back up from hips.</li><li>With a partner. Make a bridge shape. Partner goes under it. Swop.</li></ul>

Figure 2.3 Knowledge/skills/behaviours for health-related activities appropriate for 5–7 year olds

Reflective task

Reflection for early career professional

There is evidence that school programmes can successfully promote children's knowledge and behaviours about keeping healthy. How will this be planned into your provision? How will you know if this is successful?

Reflection for leader/manager

Consider how to adopt a whole school/setting approach to health for all children. In what ways will you involve families?

References

Akobeng. A. K., Ramanan, A. V., Buchan, I. and Heller, R. F. (2006) 'Effect of breast feeding on risk of coeliac disease: A systematic review and meta-analysis of observational studies'. *Archives of Disease in Childhood* 91, 39–43

Arenz, S., Ruckerl, R. Koletzko, B. and von Kries, R. (2004) 'Breast-feeding and childhood obesity-systematic review'. *International Journal of Obesity Related metabolic Disorders* 28, 1247–56

Bailey, R. P. (1999) 'Play, Health and Physical development', in T. David (ed) *Young Children Learning*. London: Paul Chapman Press

Barker, D. J. P., Forsen, T., Utela, A., Osmond, C. and Eriksson, J. G. (2001). 'Size at birth and resilience to effects of poor living conditions in adult life: Longitudinal study'. *British Medical Journal* 323, 1273–6

Barnes, J. and Freude-Lagevardi, A. (2002) *From Pregnancy to Early Childhood: Early Interventions to Enhance the Mental Health of Children and Families*. London: Mental Health Foundation

Bolling, K. Grant, G., Hamlyn, B. and Thornton, A. (2007) *Infant Feeding Survey 2005*. London: Department of Health

Brady, L. -M., Gibb, J., Henshall, A. and Lewis, J. (2008) *Play and Exercise in Early Years: Physically Active Play in Early Childhood Provision*. London: DCSF/NCB

British Nutrition Foundation. (2009) *www.nutrition.org.uk*

Bruce, T. (2005) *Early Childhood Education*, 3rd edn. Abingdon: Hodder Arnold

Campbell, S. (2004) *Watch me Grow: A Unique, 3-Dimensional Week-by Week Look at your Baby's Behaviour and Development in the Womb*. London: Carroll and Brown

David, T. (2004) 'Young children's social and emotional development', in T. Maynard and N. Thomas (eds), *An Introduction to Early Childhood Studies*. London: Sage, p. 21

Davies, M. (2003) *Movement and Dance in Early Childhood*. London: Paul Chapman

DCSF. (2007) *The Children's Plan*. London: HMSO

DCSF. (2008) *The Early Years Foundation Stage. Setting the Standards for Learning, Development and Care for children from birth to five*. Nottingham: DCSF Publications

DCSF. (2009a) *Next Steps for Early Learning and Childcare. Building on the 10-Year Strategy*. Nottingham: DCSF Publications

DCSF. (2009b) *Healthy Lives, Brighter Futures: The Strategy for Children and Young People's Health*. London: DH Publications

DCSF. (2008) Practice Guidance for the Early Years Foundation Stage. Setting the Standards for Learning, Development and Care for children from birth to five. Non-Statutory Guidance. DCSF Publications: Nottingham

de Onis, M. and Blossner, M. (1997) *WHO Global Database on Child Growth and Malnutrition*. Geneva: WHO/NUT/77.4

Department of Health. (2004a) *Choosing Health: Making Healthier Choices Easier (Public Health White Paper)*. London: Department of Health

Department of Health (2004b) *The Health Survey for England 2003*. London: HMSO

Department of Health, Department for Education and Skills. (2004) *National Service Framework for Children, Young People and Maternity Services*. London: Department of Health

Department of Health. (2008) *Healthy Weight, Healthy Lives: A Cross-Government Strategy for England*. London: Department of Health Publications

DfES. (2000) *Healthy School Lunches for Pupils in Nursery Schools/Units* Nottingham: DfES Publications

DfES/SureStart Unit. (2002*) Birth to Three Matters: A Framework to Support Children in their Earliest Years*. London: DfES

DfES. (2004) *Every Child Matters: Change for Children*. London: HMSO

Doherty, J. and Bailey, R. (2003) *Supporting Physical Development and Physical Education in the Early Years*. Buckingham: Open University Press

Doherty, J. and Whiting, M. (2004) 'Tackling childhood obesity'. *Nursery World* April, 15–22

Edwards, C., Gandini, L. and Forman, G. (eds). (1993) *The Hundred Languages of Children: The Reggio Emilia Approach to Early Childhood Education*. Norwood, NJ: Ablex

Government Office for Science. (2007) *Foresight Tackling Obesities: Future Choices – Project Report*. Department of Innovation Universities and Skills. Available from: http://www.dius.gov.uk

Greenland, P. (2006) 'Physical development', in T. Bruce (ed), *Early Childhood: A Guide for Students*. London: Sage, p. 163

Hannaford, C. (1995) *Smart Moves: Why Learning is not All in your Head*. Arlington, NJ: Great Ocean Publishers

Infant and Toddler Forum. (2009) *Food and Nutrition for the Under Threes: A Discussion Document*. Available from: *www.infantandtoddlerforum.org* (Accessed May 2009)

Harris, J. (2000) 'Health-related exercise', in R. Bailey and T. Macfayden, (eds), *Teaching Physical Education 5–11*. London: Continuum

Health Protection Agency. (2009) *A Children's Environment and Health Strategy for the UK*. Chilton, Oxon: HPA

Hodgson, J. (2001) *Mastering Movement*. London: Methuen

Janssen, I., Craig W. M., Boyce, W. F. and and Pickett, W. (2004) 'Associations between overweight and obesity with bullying behaviours in school-aged children'. *Pediatrics* 113, (5), 1187–94

Kerr, M. (2004) 'Improving the general health of people with learning disabilities'. *Advances in Psychiatric Treatment* 10, 200–6

Law, C., Power, C., Graham, H. and Merrick, D. (2007) *Obesity and Health Inequalities. Obesity Reviews* 8 (Suppl 1), 19–22. Department of Health Public Health Research Consortium

Livingstone, M. B. E., Robson, P. J., Wallace, J. M. W. and McKinley, M. C. (2003) 'How active are we? Levels of routine physical activity in children and adults'. *Proceedings of the Nutrition Society* 62, 681–701

Malaguzzi, L. (1993). No way. The hundred is there. In C. Edwards, L. Gandini, & G. Forman (eds.), *The hundred languages of children: The Reggio Emilia approach to early childhood education*. (p. vi). Norwood, NJ: Ablex Publishing

Malina, R. M., Bouchard, C. and Bar-Or. (2004) *Growth, Maturation, and Physical Activity*. Leeds: Human Kinetics

Maude, P. (2001) *Physical Children, Active Teaching: Investigating Physical Literacy.* Buckingham: Open University Press

Mellilo, R. and Leisman, G. (2004) *Neurobehavioral Disorders of Childhood: An Evolutionary Approach.* New York: Kluwer

Mental Health Foundation. (1999) *Bright Futures: Promoting Children and Young People's Mental Health.* Available from: www.mentalhealth.org.uk. (Accessed March 2009)

National Institute for Health and Clinical Excellence (NICE). (2009) *Promoting Physical Activity, Active Play and Sport for Pre-School and School-Age Children And Young People in Family, Pre-School, School and Community Settings.* London: NICE

National Audit Office. (2001) *Tackling obesity in England.* London: The Stationary Office

Ofsted. (2001) *Full Day Care: Guidance to the National Standards* London: Office for Standards in Education

Ofsted. (2005) *Early Years: Firm Foundations.* London: Ofsted

Ofsted (2006a) *Healthy Schools, Healthy Children? The Contribution of Education to Pupils' Health and Well-Being.* London: Ofsted

Ofsted. (2006b) *Food for Thought. A Survey of Healthy Eating in Registered Childcare.* London: Ofsted

Pickup, I. (2008) 'Contemporary issues and primary physical education', in I. Pickup, L. Price, J. Shaughnessy, J. Spence and M. Trace, (eds). *Achieving QTS. Meeting the Professional Standards Framework. Learning to Teach Primary PE.* Exeter: Learning Matters

McCain, M. N. and Mustard, J. F. (1999) *Early Years Study: Reversing the Real Brain Drain.* Toronto: Ontario Children's Secretatiat

Sallis, J. F. (1994) 'Determinants of Physical Activity Behavior in Children,' in R. R. Pate and R. C. Hohn (eds), *Health and Fitness through Physical Education.* Leeds: Human Kinetics

School Food Trust. Eat better Do Better. (2008) The Impact of Primary School Breakfast Clubs in Deprived Areas of London. Available from: www. schoolfoodtrust.org.uk. (Accessed January 2009)

Simeon, D. T. and Grantham-McGregor S. (1989) 'Effect of Missing Breakfast on the Cognitive Functions of School Children of Different Nutritional Status'. *American Journal of Clinical Nutrition* 49, 646–53

Soil Association. (2008) *Georgie Porgie Pudding and Pie. Exposing the Truth about Nursery Food.* Bristol: Soil Association

Sorhaindo, A. and Sabates, R. (2006) *Child Nutrition and School Life Outcomes.* Presentation in collaboration with Leon Feinstein and the ALSPAC team, Bristol. Centre for Research on the Wider Benefits of Learning. Institute of Education, University of London (Available from: *www. learningbenefits.net*)

The Caroline Walker Trust. (2009) Available from: www. cwt.org.uk/

Wanless, D. (2004) *Securing Good Health for the Whole Population: Final Report.* London: HM Treasury/Department of Health.

Wood, L. and Harper, C. (2008) *The Link Between Child Nutrition and Health: An Overview of Research in the UK.* School Food Trust. Eat Better Do Better. Available from: *www.schoolfoodtrust.org.uk.* (Accessed June 2009)

World Health Organization. (1948a) *Preamble to the Constitution of the World Health Organization as adopted by the International Health Conference,* New York, 19th June to 22nd July 1946 and entered into force 7th April 1948

World Health Organization. (1948b) *Constitution of the World Health Organization as adopted by the International Health Conference,* New York, 19th June to 22nd July 1946 and entered into force 7th April 1948

World Health Organization. (2007) What is mental health? Available from: www.who.int/topics/mental_health/en/ (Accessed March 2009)

Using Equipment and Materials

Chapter Outline

Introduction

The Early Years Foundation Stage emphasizes that it is through play that children develop intellectually, creatively, physically, socially and emotionally (The Early Years Foundation Stage. Practice Guidance, DCSF, 2008a). It talks about the importance of high quality play, tailored to individual needs, where children develop at their own pace, make friends and learn as they play. It is critically important to healthy growth, well-being, creativity and the ability to learn (ECF, 2008). Vygotsky (1978) believed that all developmental tendencies occur in play in a condensed form. Children who engage in play are happier, better adjusted, more cooperative, and more popular with their peers than those who play less (Singer, 1994). It helps to address children's emotional needs. Play is an irrefutable part of early childhood and extends across domains, ages and cultures. It involves exploration and creativity, helps flexible thinking, language skills, learning and problem-solving skills (DCSF, 2008b). Children do need time to play on their own, but they also enjoy and benefit from playing with parents and grandparents. Some of the richest play is seen when adults are involved with children as the complexity of what they do *increases substantially (Power, 2000)*. Surely now the need for intergenerational play has never been more urgent. Sharing time together and playing games with parents and grandparents hold many benefits for young and old. Family times like days in the park, on holiday, on outings or simply being together at mealtimes provide wonderful opportunities for shared play experiences. The use of equipment and materials is a crucial element of this play.

Across cultures, play objects like clothes and teddy bears can act as a bridge between a child's dependency on adults and gradual independence in the environment (Sayeed and Guerin, 2000). Play with equipment and materials develops all of the above skills and it offers children opportunities to take risks, to test their capabilities and exercise choice and control over their physical actions. There is consensus that play occupies a significant position in the lives of children. Researcher Birgitta Almqvist, in some early work with Swedish five-year-olds asked a group of children what would happen if someone told them that play was no longer allowed. After some deliberation one of the group boldly announced, 'I wouldn't care, I'd just go on playing' (1994: 50). From a number of definitions, but in our view, one that is succinct and most helpful is, 'Play is what children and young people do when they follow their own ideas and interests, in their own way and for their own reasons.' (DCMS, 2004) which seems to capture the child-centredness of this as an activity and its empowerment for children. We also like the little story provided by Elizabeth Matterson in an early work who said that play is when ' a child spends all morning making a garage for his toys, and when he is called to put his coat on to go shopping says, 'But I haven't had time to play with it yet' (1965: 3). Certain features are generally recognized as critical to defining it and we particularly welcome the attributes of play put forward by Catherine Garvey:

- Play is pleasurable and enjoyable
- Play has no extrinsic goals. Its motivations are intrinsic and serve no other objectives
- Play is spontaneous and voluntary
- Play involves some active engagement on the part of the play. (1990: 4)

The right to play for all children, supported in Article 31 of the UN Convention on the Rights of the Child and ratified in 1991 imposes a duty on local authorities to protect and promote play opportunities for children and young people of all ages, interests and abilities. Public investment in play should aim to protect children's freedom to play and to provide safe and stimulating environments that allow children to gain from the many benefits that play offers. The publication *Best Play: What provision should do for children* states 'there is a need for a variety of play provision, play areas, playgrounds, playing fields, adventure playgrounds, play centres, after school clubs and holiday playschemes, to meet the complex and diverse needs of children, families and communities' (NPFA, 2000: 15). For a number of years, play provision was afforded low status and suffered from lack of funding. Children's' free time has certainly been reduced in the last few decades and pressures to achieve academically have increased. There are anxieties from parents about the risks of play outdoors and the hectic lifestyles so many people lead nowadays had designated play as a low priority. Things are, however, changing. Recently there has been a growing recognition of the benefits of play not only to children (as we have described earlier), but to local communities. Beunderman and colleagues maintain that public space is a free and shared resource that we all draw upon (2007). Play spaces are so important and play of quality that is rewarding and enhances development requires better play facilities and opportunities. The Fair Play consultation (DCSF, 2008c) showed that children want to play outside and they also wanted better play and more exciting play environments with more challenging equipment and activities. Successful play spaces offer movement and physical activity to allow for energetic and strength building, are good for social interactions that allow choices to play alone or with others to negotiate, cooperate, compete and resolve conflicts. They should offer challenge, stimulate the senses and enable children to learn about the natural environment (Shackell et al., 2008). The recent Government's Play Strategy sets out a vision for excellent play opportunities in every local area. In developing play spaces, it advises that serious consideration must be given to issues of access, challenge and multi-sensory stimulation to cater for the needs of *all* children. The environment is crucial to meaningfully supporting inclusive play. Play environments that are truly inclusive offer opportunities for exploration and discovery of open – ended destinations while dull or neglected environments result in frustration or destruction (Casey, 2005). Drawing on the work of Hughes (1999) and others, we offer the following criteria for rich inclusive play environments using equipment and materials

- are accessible to all – meets the needs and interests of children and the community;
- offers variety – different sized spaces, includes places to hide and places to reflect and inspire. Surfaces protect and equipment intrigues
- provides degrees of safe challenge – tests and when appropriate extends capability in a safe framework;
- are multi-sensory – to stimulate all five senses;
- includes natural elements and man-made materials;
- promotes vigorous physical activity – with opportunities to move, balance, swing, climb, etc.
- takes account of changes and evolution;

Budget and funding constraints among other factors, have led to a reduction in places for children to play that are safe, and at the same time intrigue and offer them sufficient challenge. Where are the play spaces that children are excited to go to and that will be lasting memories for them? Since the early 1980s over 5,000 playing fields have been sold off. Adult worries about safety have led to a gradual diminishing of outdoor play spaces for children so much so that writers like O'Brien et al. (2000) propose that letting children play outdoors is becoming a marker for parental irresponsibility. What a sad indictment of our society. Every child has the right to experience and enjoy the very special benefits of being outdoors. Sue Palmer (2006) talks of being in the outdoors as 're-establishing children's right to roam' (p. 62) and 'extending their free-range existence' (p. 63). Being outdoors is one of the most enduring joys of childhood. Outdoor learning provides unique opportunities for children to use all their senses, to be thrilled at the new scale it offers and the sense of freedom it brings. New sights and smells provide immediate and valuable ways for babies to understand this environment and linked to cognitive development provides important kinaesthetic paths to learning (Goswami, 2004). In the physical domain it is seen when children want to try physical activities for enjoyment and master gross motor skills like running, jumping and climbing, mastering fine motor skills like mark-making and posting shapes in boxes (Anning, 1991). Learning experienced outdoors should complement those in the indoors and when appropriate, extend it. It is an excellent medium for cross-curricular learning, making it relevant and exciting for children. Table 3.1 gives some practical examples of how the use of equipment outdoors can provide appropriate challenge for children within the EYFS.

Table 3.1 Use of equipment outdoors to provide challenge for children in the EYFS

Area of Learning	Activities with equipment and materials
Personal, Social & Emotional Development	Treasure baskets with a range of natural materials and everyday objects; physical achievements (e.g. balancing on a plank for the first time); parachute games that build trust and co-operation; planting seeds; visits to shops to buy foods from around the world; picnics; collaborating to make a den
Communication, Language & Literacy	Dressing up to act out stories; Lotto games to improve listening; making music with musical instruments; reading and making signs in the outdoors; following maps; using clipboards to write in role play (e.g. hospitals); mark-making; reading print in the environment.
Problem-Solving, Reasoning & Numeracy	Number walks; counting out equipment; chalking numbers on the ground for playground games; estimations, e.g. 'Who has the most conkers?'; 'How many cups are there…'; patterns in brickwork; using timers to record time take to negotiate obstacles courses and trails; money and cash tills.
Knowledge & Understanding of the World	Mini-beast hunts; planting bulbs; weaving using natural materials; natural sculpting; using digital cameras to record walks in the local environment; the use of props in multi-cultural festivals e.g. Dragon dance, Diwali; using radio-controlled cars and battery operated equipment.
Physical Development	Obstacle courses; treasure hunts; den building; using large climbing apparatus; using stop watches; water and sand play; games equipment like quoits, beanbags, hoops and balls to travel, send and receive; negotiating pathways with various wheeled vehicles.
Creative Development	Observational drawings; mixing colours; printing; bark rubbings; collages; weaving with strings, twigs raffia, etc; moving to taped music; modelling; using musical instruments.

The outdoors offers special opportunities to promote children's physical skills and satisfy their sense of adventure. It is now recognized as integral to quality continuous provision and not separated out as timetabled outdoor play (see research by Gura (1992) which showed that children left block play activities indoors to get outside, thereby abandoning this learning resulting in a 'hit and run' approach to play). As Lasenby (1990) reminds, indoors and outdoors should be viewed as linked where children move between the two

Photograph 3.1 Using equipment (© P. Hopkins)

using equipment and resources to best fit their needs and where the play requires them (1990: 5). Such a joined up approach also necessitates the two having equal status and valued by adults as well as children. We recently witnessed a lovely example in a Nursery where some children were planning a wedding. They used clothes from the dressing up box, gave each child a role to play and then the bride and groom promptly went outside into the 'wedding car' awaiting them. The outdoor provides many opportunities to involve adults. Commitment 3.3 in the EYFS supports enabling outdoor environments that support children's health, well-being and development due to the confidence it provides from exploring and learning in secure yet challenging spaces. Margaret Edgington (2001) advises them to be educators, not supervisors and to be involved alongside the children, saying that adults who are talking to each other are shivering or bored give children no idea how to develop their interests. She recommends involvement through observing and noting progress, extending children ideas when they play, setting up equipment to challenge, organizing appropriate games and initiating activities such as bulb planting.

Keeping children safe both outdoors and indoors is of the highest priority for all those who work with children. Common potential hazards in homes and settings are likely to include stairs, doors, medicines, car seats, scissors and knives, electricity points and cupboard doors. All providers need to conduct a formal risk assessment and constantly reappraise environments and activities and make adjustments to secure children are safe at all times. It is important that equipment is safe and that all necessary safety precautions and risk assessments are carried out regularly and diligently. Adults have a responsibility to protect children from hazards and provide them with safe play environments that offer challenging opportunities to explore, practise and gain new levels of competency. Autistic children have little understanding of danger and practitioners need to supervize and be vigilant when equipment like scissors are used. They need to ensure too that there are no unstable pieces of furniture that could be pulled over or climbed on and it is advisable to have safety surfaces under large pieces of outdoor apparatus like climbing frames.

There is evidence that a degree of risk is necessary and a connection between risk assessment and learning. Removing all hazards from our lives is neither possible nor desirable impossible since it also becomes challenge free. Children do benefit from exposure to risks with challenges to help develop skills and confidence and ensuring that unnecessary risks are minimized (NICE, 2009). It increases independence and learning and children can be seriously disadvantaged if they do not learn how to manage both physical and emotional risks and is particularly pertinent where equipment is concerned. This issue is explored further in the box below.

Case study

My 3-year old (boy) left the UK relatively inexperienced. Three months in New Zealand saw him really ready to explore challenges he was presented with. Also, having equipment beyond his physical scope taught him when something was too dangerous yet' This is a comment from a parent in the review *Getting Serious about*

⇨

Case study—Cont'd

Play (DCMS, 2004: 13) that sums up the way in which children (and in this case boys) are quite capable at assessing risk for themselves. Research tells us that children manage situations that involve chance and risk on a daily basis well. We know too, that from early childhood boys engage in more risk taking than girls (Rosen and Peterson, 1990) – a fact reflected in the birth to 5 years and beyond.

Integral to such risk taking behaviours are those associated with equipment. Climbing in 'dangerous' places or racing around outdoor areas on wheeled vehicles in what often is viewed by adults as recklessly, are common occurrences. Part of play is about excitement and it doesn't take some children long to discover where the places that offer them most excitement are or how to use equipment to satisfy this desire for thrill and adventure. When using equipment, babies require constant supervision as their understanding of potential risk is limited or non-existent. Play environments involving equipment, should involve pre-school children in assessing risks and making decisions about their actions. Judgements improve with experience and are best promoted by giving responsibility, experimentation within safe frameworks and balanced with clear instructions about how to use equipment safely. Avery and Jackson (1993) found that involving children and teaching them to use equipment safely helped in reducing accidents. Their study found that it was when there were children of different ages together on equipment that accidents were most likely to occur.

Reflection for early career professional

If we recognize that every child is a competent learner from birth who can be resilient, capable, confident and self assured, how would a practitioner promote that sense of exploration and risk taking in the physical domain?

Reflection for leader/manager

Scenario. It has arisen that staff in the setting have concerns about children's safety outdoors. When you meet as a staff team, what measures need to be taken to resolve this issue?

Development of equipment and materials through play and exploration

It is generally accepted (e.g. writers like Hughes, 1999; Isenberg and Jalango, 2000) among others, that early exposure to appropriate play materials provide a sound basis through which to promote children's development. Careful consideration must be given to equipment and materials so that the needs of every child regardless of ability or disability are fully supported. Children who might be naturally shy, are overweight or have coordination difficulties will require more support and encouragement so their play is fulfilling and rewarding. When play materials and equipment are of high quality, this is often reflected in the quality of play observed. Play with objects links the child with the environment immediately and directly, operating as a medium for the expression of feelings or interests, providing a channel for social interaction with adults or peers. This is not a new idea. One hundred years ago, an early pioneer of the kindergarten movement, Friedrich Froebel saw play as a unifying force between children, adults and the environment (1906). Play with unfamiliar objects sets up a chain of exploration, familiarization and later understanding. This repeated sequence leads to developing conceptions of the properties of the physical world such as shape, texture and size (Garvey, 1990). An important sequence becomes established with objects and materials: exploration and discovery leading to manipulation and play. Let us illustrate this point. In the first 6 months children explore objects such as rattles and shakers which, after some investigation with hands and even feet, usually end up in their mouths for further analysis. In the next 6 months objects are explored with much more purpose and familiar toys and other objects are played with as a solitary enterprise. From 6 to 10 months on average, infants begin to understand the concept of 'object permanence' – in other words when an object is out of sight it is literally out of mind. Parents who go along with the game of picking up the rattle off the floor again and again while the child happily drops it repeatedly are strengthening their child's understanding of object permanence. From 12 to 24 months, in the stage of parallel play children play alongside other children. They may well use the same toys and materials but do not interact with each other. Between 2 and 3 years, is the advent of cooperative play and turn-taking with other children and we see behaviours of social pretend play like dressing up and pretend cooking and constructive play such as building models with Lego bricks. Associative play occurs from the age of four and may involve children sharing materials, often working together to complete a project such as building a den. As children get older, their play with objects undergoes changes. There is an increased intellectual contribution as cognitive structures develop and experiences widen. Models become more intricate and make use of a greater range of materials. Games become more complex as rule structures are incorporated and demand different equipment. Imaginative capabilities allow for more sophistication, for example in the use of props in dramatic play.

Play with toys has a special function for children and has a history dating back to the earliest times. Children who have access to a variety of toys were found to reach higher levels of intellectual achievement (Elardo et al., 1975). Children sustain their play for longer periods when there is a range of toys available to them. Their properties, realism, mechanical complexity and the relationship to home or adventure have bearing on their value as imaginative play (Singer, 1994). They also need to be safe, affordable and developmentally appropriate (Glassy and Romano, 2003). That is not to say that play materials and toys need to be elaborate and costly. Often the reverse is true. Overly complex and sophisticate toys can constrain children's imagination. How many parents have bought their children expensive toys and have watched with dismay as the child seemed more interested in the cardboard box than the contents! Simple toys can stimulate imaginative play very well. Old hats, coats, shoes and handbags are ideal to stimulate imaginative play in the dressing up area very well. A plastic pizza can only ever be a plastic pizza. Materials and often natural ones like sand, clay and pebbles can fuel children's imagination in exciting ways. A block of wood can instantly become a mobile phone, a stick can become a light sabre. A dressing gown can become a flowing royal robe. A basket of conkers can serve as money or food. Domestic items such as saucepan lids, pegs and washing baskets have untold uses in children's play – because children use them in imaginative ways. Old blankets have been transformed into dens, to castles, forts and to secret private places allowing children to construct their own worlds of fantasy and fun. Singer (cited in Goldstein, 1994) reports a study by Mary Ann Pulaski (1973) who used minimally structured toys that included drawing paper, paints, blocks, pipe-cleaners and dressing up materials and found play was richer and more varied than when structured play materials like as a Service Station, a metal doll's house, dolls and specific outfits for the dolls like an astronaut's suit and a bride's dress were made available. Similarly a later study reported by Singer with 4 and 5 year olds, observed that dressing up materials, puppets and stuffed animals were used more often in social pretend play than puzzles, small blocks and colouring materials (Connolly et al., 1988). The National Association of Toy and Leisure Libraries publishes annually their *Good Toy Guide* (2009) which shows the benefits and skills promoted by different toys.

Play culture for boys and girls differs and the differences are consistent over-time and across cultures (Gussin-Paley, 1984). Infant males prefer mechanical and structural toys and look at these for shorter, more active periods than girls do. Boys' playground games in the pre-school years favour vigorous and competitive activities. When they play with blocks, boys of this age build high tower-like structures that are likely to topple, in contrast to girls whose playground games are quieter and less active. When they play with blocks, girls tend to build low and long structures (Gurian, 2001). The potential for materials like blocks to enhance learning is widely recognized among practitioners and also in research. In *Writing in the Air,* its capacity to build boys' oral and later writing skills is strongly presented (Marin, 2004). Research identifies gender differences in children's play and preferences of sex-typed toys typically attributed to gender group identification and social learning. More recent research also attributes this to biological factors. Alexander and Hines (2002), for example suggest innate sex differences contribute to a 'biological preparedness' for objects such as toys that prepare children for either 'masculine' or 'feminine' gender roles, which develops alongside gender socialization. Due to processing differences in colour, shape and movement, girls are more attracted by round, softly coloured objects, while boys prefer moving objects (Alexander, 2003). Exposure to visual and auditory stimuli from an early age for children is essential (Murata and Maeda, 2002). For boys and girls, playing with toys and play materials provide vital experiences to match and compare colours, shapes, sizes and sounds and assist understanding of spatial concepts. Pans and cups and other utensils found in the home, even furniture help with understanding volume. Dolls, dressing up clothes, musical instruments and mark-making and writing materials facilitate language, imitation and self-expression as important aspects of development.

Photograph 3.2 Playing with wooden blocks

Play with different equipment and materials then is an excellent way to promote children's all round development. Recently, we had the privilege to observe two 5 year olds, Tina and Harry playing with wooden blocks on the floor of a Nursery and observed this in action. The children were playing alongside each other and as we listened we could hear the children talking to themselves and at times to each other. Tina was building an elaborate road way structure with impressive curves and straight sections. Harry had decided to build a tower-type structure that allowed him to run a toy car up and down the ramps he had built. In this brief episode, we saw intense concentration and determination as expressions of intellectual engagement. Language expression was evident; there was social interaction and physicality. For ten minutes this was their entire world and a world that totally absorbed them. This was their work and their pleasure and represented everything that defines children's play: self-expression, communication, self-appointed engagement, discovery and sheer enjoyment. Central to this play was the way in which the children set the agenda for their own play. They were the ones who set the rules and the goals, not adults. Ownership of the rules also meant being able to change those rules too. In play like this, this often involves the use of negotiating skills and appropriate language. Children's learning is extended when the boundaries of their play are explored and even pushed, when they use resources in different ways and they do not feel constrained by time, routines or even the weather! A good example of the latter appears on the EYFS CD-ROM (3.3 – Playing with sand and water). It is a rainy day. Rain is dripping through the umbrella on to a sandpit. Two boys and a practitioner, appropriately dressed, are exploring the effect of the dripping water dripping onto their buckets of sand. Take a look at this. Do you think this scenario tells us something about how children use and play with the resources? Using equipment in play allows children to engage in 'what if?' type activities and following an interest or line of enquiry that is significant to them. What if I keep dropping my rattle on the floor? Will mummy always pick it up? What if I use the hammer in my other hand to bang in these pegs? What if I put another beaker on the top of the others in my tower? Will they all fall down? Such questions allow children to set their own goals and when things do go wrong, receive feedback so that important lessons to be learned.

Equipment can be a powerful vehicle to assist learning in play. Open-ended play is play without restrictions and has no 'right' or 'wrong' answers. This type of play allows for exploration and for children to be free without pressure to 'get it right'. In this free flow play (Bruce, 1991), there is no one answer or single outcome. How can the imagination and generation of ideas involved in building a den with some wood and a sheet to create a child's very own special place possibly be quantified? What is play and what is learning is extremely difficult to separate. A 3 year old experimenting with some plastic cups becomes absorbed in sorting, classifying and comparing them. Is this play or is it learning? Children do not distinguish between play and learning: adults seem to. In their play, they are laying down essential building blocks of future learning and decades of documented research underscore the contribution that play brings to the lives of children from infancy through to adolescence. Increasing advances in neuroscience underscore the importance of play and learning and highlight how active brains make vital neuronal connections from being born that are critical to learning. Thus, the experiences children have in those early formative years are so vital. We are mindful of Bloom's early work when he reported that 80 per cent of all learning at 18 years is attained through play by 8 years and that 50 per cent was attained by age 4 years through play (1964). Babies experience the world through their senses and learn primarily through movements. This continues with maturity, learning through experience and action. EYFS Card 4.2 on active learning refers to children learning best through physical and mental challenges. Active learning it says, involves other people, objects, ideas and events that engage and involve children for sustained periods. Watching an adult skilfully using scissors in a cutting activity can inspire a child to want to learn how to master this skill and copy the adult. Competence leads to success and to enjoyment and increased confidence. Children can use equipment in a positive way in their relationships with peers. Sharing toys with others, learning to wait and take turns, cooperating and working out differences are some examples of how equipment is integral to childhood friendships and the notion of being a friend (see research by Newcomb and Bagwell, 1995).

When they play and use apparatus and equipment, they are learning new skills and practicing existing ones. Play provides the most appropriate support for scaffolding skills and is better than in any other context (Guddemi et al., 1999). For the toddler of 18 months the skill of holding a spoon and using it to eat with consistent success is a challenge to be mastered as is being able to ride around obstacles in a playground on a bike for the older child. Equipment can be an important way for adults and children to share experiences. A steadying hand when learning to ride a bike, cooking together or playing with a ball are all vital shared natural experiences with adults and peers that are fun and have huge educational value. Equipment must be matched to individual developmental needs. Spend 5 minutes in a Reception class when the children are using bats and balls outdoors, exploring what the equipment does and what they can do with the equipment. You will notice immediately the variances in height and weight of the group. Look again and you will see a few of the children moving awkwardly with the equipment and experiencing difficulties in controlling the ball. Others appear confident and competent and are already demonstrating their skill in handling and using the equipment. Physically the children are at different stages of maturation and at different stages in their movement mastery. Differences in the levels of skill in this activity are obvious. Developmentally appropriate practices in this scenario require an informed practitioner who uses knowledge of how children develop to take account of individual differences and provides a range of sizes, weights and shapes of bats and balls to ensure that *every* child is successful and finds the experience rewarding. Writing about the connection between physical play and skill development, Trish Maude tells us that, 'play provision should take account of play limitations as well as capabilities, the power of play in facilitating motor skills acquisition and in providing endless opportunities for practice, repetition and refinement of physical skills' (2001: 29). Werner and Burton (1979) remind us that active learning requires an appropriate physical environment and one that stimulates the child's curiosity and desire to explore and engage. For babies, this means a safe, clean environment with play materials that meets their specific needs. Older children enjoy developing their skills in safe environments with different equipment that facilitates the development of their skills and offers them a degree of challenge.

As discussed earlier, is physical activity play, which has a significant role in helping to increase levels of physical activity in children. It follows then that as a strategy to counter the rise in obesity figures in children, encouraging children to participate in physical activity play outdoors holds much merit. Physical activity play burns more calories than any other form of play and physical play outdoors burns more calories than corresponding play indoors (Pellegrini et al., 1998). Having regular physical activity in the early years lays solid foundations for maintaining active lifestyles throughout children's lives. Sedentary lifestyles and increased calorific intake of foods high in saturated fats have led children in Marjorie Ouvry's lovely words 'into being couch potatoes instead of runner beans' (2003: 13). Many traditionally 'adult' diseases, such as posture problems. stress, anxiety, high blood pressure are now increasingly evident in younger children. When play involves physical engagement with equipment, as it did in the examples above, it has a valuable contribution to make to promoting children's physical development. It helps develop gross motor skills – skipping with a rope, using bikes and trikes, balancing on top of planks above the ground, crawling through barrels and tunnels, climbing up and down steps and swinging from apparatus build strength, flexibility and endurance and help with coordination and body awareness. Fine motor skills are developed in Small World play, threading beads, using construction materials like Duplo, building with blocks, playing with playdough, hammering shapes into pegboards and using real tools, pouring water and sand into different sized containers. Cutting with scissors, mark-making with chalks and paint brushes, sprinkling glitter and simply holding pencils are excellent ways to help developing fine motor control. Hand-eye coordination is improved by bouncing and throwing and catching balls of different shapes and sizes and striking balls with bats. Manipulative skills are improved through imaginative play by dressing up, fasting zips and doing and undoing buttons, dialling on mobile phones, writing cards, lists and invitations, wrapping presents and by pretend cooking.

Using equipment and materials from birth to 3 years of age

Historically, the youngest children were viewed as 'tabula rasa', blank slates who were vulnerable and dependent on others, driven only by immediate physical and emotional needs. Modern developmental and neurobiological research findings indicate that this is highly inaccurate. New evidence has emerged that provides startling insights that have gradually transformed the

Photograph 3.3 Physical Play in the First 3 Years (Photography by L Nahmd-Williams)

outdated view to one of the infant and young child as a capable learning machine. Elinor Goldschmied (1994) refers to our youngest children as 'people under three' which suggests that, from birth, they are at a unique period in development and recognizes the very earliest years as a life stage with its own integrity.

Play is a crucially important activity for babies and toddlers, helping them make sense of their world, express how they feel and form relationships with those around them. How they use materials and equipment is integral to promoting this development. *Birth to Three Matters: A Review of the Literature* (David et al., 2003; DfES, 2002) made it clear when it reminded that, 'Play of course soon becomes the contextual space where meaning is made and negotiated as children develop ways of interacting with toys, space and 'others' to construct and reconstruct worlds' (p. 91). It is through play that children express who they are through their 'hundred languages' by dancing, music making, painting, gardening, making patterns, building, model-making, 'animating' puppets and other toys and dressing up. As they become more skilful and acquire more sophisticated language they talk about and share what they know in different ways, such as the things they paint, draw and play with. Babies discover mark-making by chance, noticing that when they put their hand in wet sand their print stays there. They begin to recognize some marks and realize these mean something to others (DfES, 2002).

A form of play commonly seen with 1–3 year olds is 'heuristic play' (Goldschmied, 1987) – early exploratory play with objects like boxes, jars and various types of containers. Heuristic play offers an insight into how collections of objects can facilitate first-hand experience of treasures from the real world, through exploring what they can and cannot do (Doherty et al., 2009). Here the focus of this play is on discovery, finding out about objects by manipulating them, filling and emptying them and putting things in and out of them. There is much is supportive and facilitatory – collecting a range of objects to stimulate the child and observing the play (Doherty et al., 2009). Everyday non-commercial objects like corks, ribbons, tubes, pegs are ideal to support children's self-exploration and discovery. It was Elinor Goldschmied (1987) who promoted heuristic play and pioneered treasure baskets as a result of her observations of young children playing with objects from the real world.

Case study

Goldschmied's observations of babies and young children revealed how they were fascinated by everyday objects like wooden spoons, saucepans and bottles. She discovered that babies concentrated and persevered in their play with these natural objects. Her treasure baskets were made from natural wicker filled with objects found in the home, none of which were commercially manufactured toys. Baskets, draw bags and small boxes of natural 'treasure' are frequently seen in many early years settings today to promote multi-sensory play. The objects normally vary in size, shape, temperature, colour, texture, smell and taste to encourage play and investigation. Feathers, pegs, lids, metal objects, cotton reels, cloth, sponges with different textures and wooden shapes are ideal for this age group. Indeed there is evidence that children's concentration levels are higher when they play with natural objects in a treasure basket than with manufactured toys (Goldschmied and Jackson, 2004). Through heuristic play, practitioners can explore the learning skills and needs of young children (Hughes, 2006) and extend their thinking.

Sarah-Jane, the birth-to-three coordinator in a Children's Centre told us how one room at the Centre is dedicated to heuristic play. In this room there are a number of baskets with different objects made from natural resources. The key workers vary the objects according to the children's interests and schema. Since introducing Treasure baskets and spending time watching how the babies interact with them, practitioners feel that the quality of their observations have improved significantly.

Practical task for early career professional

Set up several Treasure baskets for the youngest learners in your setting. Carefully consider the content of the baskets. How might the baskets be integrated into your existing provision? Now evaluate how effective they were.

Practical task for leader/manager

Set up several Treasure baskets for the youngest learners in your setting. Monitor the use of treasure baskets in the setting over 4 weeks: who uses them, how often they are used, how often contents are altered by staff. Are their observable changes in the quality of adult-child relationships and/or verbal interactions from using the baskets?

Play and cognitive development are connected. At play, children show greater evidence of problem-solving abilities and creativity. Findings from neuroscience have given us new insights into how young children learn and affirm them as competent learners from birth. The brain fuels learning. It increases in weight three times by the end of a child's first year and continues to expand. By age 3, it is 75 per cent of adult weight. Alongside growth increases in the physical size of the brain (think of this as the brain's 'hardware') developing cerebral processes (think of these as 'software') are making vital connections and it is through these experiences that learning takes place. The most intense period for these connections takes place over the first 3 years, as a result of the interplay of heredity and environment. Nature and nurture working together. Early stimulation is essential if learning is to be maximized and play, providing opportunities for problem-solving, making choices and reaching decisions is an ideal vehicle to do this. In imaginative play children re-enact familiar scenes and stories with props and other resources. They imitate and improvize what they have observed – for one child a block of wood is now a truck and for another a scarf soon becomes a cloak and the fantasy begins. Piaget's description of how children process information actively from first hand experiences underpins most constructivist perspectives on learning (Anning and Edwards, 1999). Although his descriptions of ages and stages are not wholly accurate, his notion of schema is a critically important concept in helping us understand just how our youngest children perceive their world. Objects soon become significant for young children. They need objects of different textures, sizes, shapes and colours to explore. They enjoy watching moving objects. Mobiles and contrasting patterns places in a baby's cot offer visual stimulation and they will lie absorbed for long periods watching them. Between 4 and 9 months, movements are initiated to make things happen. When a baby holds a rattle and shakes it, the child finds out that it makes a particular sound that other objects do not make. It has a certain feel, a certain heaviness and so on. Schemas connect objects and ideas together: a *pair* of socks or a *big* teddy. Objects linked to learning are significant and as we discussed earlier with Treasure baskets.

From their first moments, babies communicate needs and feelings through movement and this is a powerful mechanism for learning. They use movement and sensory exploration to connect with their immediate environment and respond to what they can see, hear, feel, touch and smell. They are seen to be busily engaged in stacking, tipping, pouring, gathering, filling and dismantling all manner of household objects and play materials. Under-threes are active learners, equipped to make sense of the plethora of information that bombards their senses and endeavouring to become mobile, independent beings. For babies, safe-crawl areas should be created and objects made available for them to investigate and enjoy. In the early stages of walking they use furniture to hold onto to help them balance and push carts and even boxes. Later, wheeled vehicles, like Kiddie cars, pushcarts large lorries and trikes enhance mobility and involve the whole body in continuity of motion. Hodgson emphasizes this in stating that 'everything that we discover about life, we discover through movement' (2001: 172). Movement helps make neuronal connections in several regions of the learning brain – the basal ganglia, cerebellum and corpus callosum. It helps put ideas into action to accomplish a goal. When 13 month old Raz sees the fluffy teddy bear in front of her she reaches out to grasp it. Her first attempt overextends (the goal) and the second is too short but on the third she successfully takes hold of the bear. Here, motivation combined with perceptual, cognitive and physical development in her response to the task, the individual and the environment combine to achieve learning through movement (Doherty and Bailey, 2003).

Ours is a social world and children are 'hard wired' to engage in activities that develop their abilities to understand and respond to the feelings of others. Social play is a key mechanism for early learning (Creasey et al., 1998). This early period is when they begin the process of understanding social intercourse and by the end of this time some children demonstrate sharing, taking turns and cooperating. Equipment such as toys can facilitate this process well. Young children begin to play games and cooperate in playing games from 18 months and games of increased complexity and rules, help to promote this. Research by Dunn (2004) shows how friendships with other young children are seen through reciprocity, recognition and affection. Babies feel secure with adults who are responsive to their needs and tune into their interests, such as parents, carers and their key worker in settings. Periods of play with toys and objects become times to share in the delights of everyday events or achievements and times for adults and infants to get to know each other. A soft fluffy toy becomes a way of connecting the adult to the child and can be a useful way to introduce an unfamiliar face and build confidence and trust. Toys and objects in everyday situations can promote learning, movement and social skills in a most immediate way. Take this example of Kari in her bath.

Case study

It was bath time for 11 month old Kari. Her mother gently lowered her in and she immediately reached for the bright measuring spoon floating in the water and started chewing on it. Then she slapped the spoon up and down in the water. Her mum splashed the water. Kari splashed again and looked up at her mum. Then they both splashed the water and laughed. A blue plastic duck caught her attention and Kari grabbed for this, letting go of the spoon. The spoon dropped into the water and sank below the surface. Interested in what she saw, Tanya dropped the duck and reached under the water for the spoon. She let it go so it fell into the water. She watched it sink and then picked it up again. Kari's mum put some soap onto a sponge and began to sing their special bath song, 'Head and shoulders, knees and toes, knees and toes . . .' Kari laughed, splashed her hands down into the bath and cooed with delight.

Reflection

After reading the story, did you get a sense of the close bond between Kari and her mother? Did you see how objects featured significantly in the adult-child interaction?

Could you tell how important the environment was in promoting this interaction? Young children do more than interact with their environments; they absorb them! The right type of environments have secure surroundings and equipment to meet individual needs and support development. When children feel secure about their surroundings, they are motivated to explore them. Its importance impacts upon the quality of practice and one that practitioners need to plan for and review regularly. The excellent *Creating Places for Birth to Threes* from Community Playthings (2005, pp. 12–13) contains a cornucopia of useful advice and practical ideas about furnishing spaces both indoors and outdoors. Practical suggestions are included in Table 3.2.

Table 3.2 Equipment for the under three's

Age in months	Appropriate equipment
0–6 months	Cots
	Room dividers to screen sleep area
	Nappy-changing unit
	Glider, rocking chair, or settee for feeding and bonding
	Table for bottles
	Treasure basket
	Baby floor gym and mat
6–12 months	Chairs with trays and/or
	Low table and chairs
	Mirrors
	Treasure baskets containing variety of tactile objects
	Shelves to store treasure baskets
	Book display units accessible to babies
	Objects to push (cartons, sturdy chairs, pushcarts)
	Nursery gym
	Objects to crawl through and cruise around
12–24 months	Trolley for food and dishes
	Sand & water table
	Low easels
	Low tables and small chairs
	Wide range of everyday objects
	Nursery gym
	Wheeled riding toys
	Rocking equipment
	Push carts
	Little figures of people and animals
	Small vehicles
	Floor cushions
24–36 months	Sand & water table
	Easels
	Tables
	Chairs
	oddler town
	Kiddie cars
	Small tricycles
	Small scooters
	Pushcarts
	Rocking equipment
	Hollow blocks
	Little figures of people and animals
	Materials for creating houses, fences, etc
	Small vehicles and car tracks
	Dress-up unit

Using equipment and materials from 3 to 5 years of age

Advances in all round development between 3 and 5, mean that children continue to explore their environments with enthusiasm, interact with others and accelerate their need to be physically active. Rudimentary movement patterns are secure and added mobility allows them to navigate new and further afield environments. We now witness increased strength, better coordination and a range of improved physical skills. Running, jumping and climbing become sources of delight for children of this age and they are eager to show off their prowess. This is a time in which most children enjoy testing their improved capabilities. The challenge of adults and practitioners is to be able to respond to children's need to move and to develop it event further. They are still learning how to keep themselves safe and exploration and discovery still feature highly in their play. They use equipment and toys in ways manufacturers could never envisage. Keeping a balance between safe play (especially with large equipment) and managing risk is a delicate one as we have stated, since it is impossible to remove all risk, yet desirable that play is also interesting and challenging.

Resourcing areas for play does not always correspond to the learning or use anticipated by the practitioner. In research by Wood and Bennett (1997), for instance, they found that children ignored the role play context and made up their own themes. Instead of the shop, the children changed to guard dogs and burglars! Well thought out use of resources can really improve children's use of areas in a setting and accelerate their development. In the home-corner, equipment becomes used as dressing up, preparing meals, using a computer or telephone and acting out scenarios like hospitals, in an office, a Garage, etc. The music corner should contain a range of musical instruments from different countries; resources to make patterns and collages, mixing paints or painting pictures, gluing and sticking and are essential for creative development. Sand and water invite opportunities for measuring, weighing and assist language development while manipulation and sharing tools helps fine motor and cooperative development.

Photograph 3.4 Physical Activity in Role Play; crawling through a hole (Photography by L Nahmd-Williams)

Findings from *the Play in the Early Years* study (Brady et al., 2008) showed more play took place *without* equipment than with. In the sample of 19 children, 41 per cent of all observed minutes included physically active play *without* equipment and 21 per cent included physically active play *with* equipment. Analysis of the time children were involved in physically active play, there was some *without* equipment recorded in 77 per cent, and some *with* equipment in 40 per cent of such 'active' minutes, on average. The qualitative data shows that equipment used *indoors* included a wide range of equipment – musical instruments, dolls, puppets, cars and train sets, bricks and Lego, tools, phones, pictures, puzzles, climbing frames, Wendy houses, toy furniture, dressing up clothes, sandpits and a water table, craft tools and a computer. Children also made use of furniture in their inside play, for example climbing on tables and chairs, hiding under furniture, wrapping a curtain around themselves, picking up a cushion or (for younger children) pulling themselves up holding on to a gate or table. Interesting to note that these activities and the equipment mentioned were not recorded on planning sheets. This has got implications for recording accurate pictures of the extent of children's physical activity and the equipment they use as part of this. Equipment used *outside* included bicycles, tricycles and a four-wheeled cycle, buggies, pushchairs, prams and cars, climbing frames with swings, ropes and slides, a see-saw, stilts, planks, gardening space and watering cans, bats and balls, a Wendy house and shop, a den and a tee-pee, craft materials and assorted toys.

In the context of the EYFS play-based environments, children find many avenues to express themselves and represent their feelings and ideas. Mark-making is a natural medium as part of this representation and one that takes place from a very early age. As an activity it allows their thinking to become visible and to extend it. They love the sensation of felt pens on shiny paper, of using chalks on the playground, of watching paint drip onto coloured paper to make patterns. It is a satisfying physical experience and one that develops their creativity, problem-solving and thinking skills and physical dexterity. Fine motor skills are required in mark-making since the ability to manipulate crayons and a range of other mark-making implements is essential. Fine motor control in fingers and hands to hold and direct such implements are improved and the acquisition of the pincer grip around 3+, allows for more intricate mark-making.

Moving towards Key Stage 1, the requirements to make meaningful marks (through activities such as drawing, recording, writing, etc.) for different audiences and purposes increases, both indoors and outdoors. Activities indoors might include self registration, using the White boards, the role play area as an office to fill in forms and take telephone messages, the Small world area for map-making, writing invitations, using shaving foam to 'write' with a finger on table tops, etc. Outdoors using mud and twigs, chalking on the ground, using large sheets of paper, spray painting and quiet times to write under a Gazebo. In settings resources for mark-making should be well organized and offer choice to foster children's independence and motivate them to try out new experiences. Many settings have permanent mark-making areas outdoors that can quickly linked to children's interests. Portable trollies allow a greater range of materials to be used and take learning directly from indoors to outdoors. You may wish to use some of the following:

- Crayons, marker pens, coloured pencils
- Stamps and inks
- Clipboards
- Name cards
- Chalks
- Large sheets of lining paper

- Masking tape, glues, hole punches, staplers
- Paint brushes of various widths and rollers
- Sponges and mops
- Notebooks and pads
- Diaries
- Twigs, feathers, sticks
- Shaving foam, dough and clay
- Glitter pens
- Timetables, adverts and leaflets
- OHP paper and dry-wipe pens

Home support for equipment and materials

The Home Learning Environment (HLE) is a measure of the extent to which parents take part in learning activities with their children. There is strong evidence of the beneficial impact of parental engagement on outcomes for children. It was a key finding from the EPPE study (Sylva et al., 2003). The Children's Plan (DCSF, 2007) states that parental engagement is the single most important determinant of children's achievement at school. Families can improve their child's outcomes by what they do with their child through a stimulating early home learning environment. Children with a positive HLE at the age of 3 or 4 years have been found to achieve better in the early years and throughout primary school. While the effect of background characteristics on reading and maths achievement diminishes as children grow older, the impact of the quality of the HLE still has very strong effects on academic outcomes at the ages of seven (Sammons et al., 2004). A friend recounted a story that illustrates the importance of the home and parental engagement beautifully. Grandparents, Theresa and Peter were horse-racing fans and enjoyed going to race meetings with their 5 year old granddaughter Marie. At home they watched the racing together on television and talked about the colours that the jockey wore, how the races started and what the betting odds meant. They recounted a time when Marie was painting and produced a wonderful picture of a running horse (coinciding with the time when Marie was exploring motion schema) and how she talked about how the horse's head was raised and the position of the front and hind legs of the horse running. Not long after this, Theresa and Peter were amazed another day to find that

Marie had lined up 20 toy horses on the lounge floor and was playing out a race the three had recently watched on TV. Marie also talked accurately about the odds of the horses with words like 'even money', 'odds-on favourite' and counted out the horses in sequence from 1 to 20.

Two areas that illustrate this are in early writing/mark-making and in maths which are explored in the boxes below. First, a supportive home environment is an ideal environment for mark-making to flourish as the story of 5 year old Samantha reveals.

Case study

Samantha had recently started in the Reception class at her local Primary school and already her skills at making meaningful marks were well developed. Her parents had encouraged this from being a toddler and there was always a selection of crayons, paints, pens and pencils at home for her to choose. What appeared as scribbles around 2 years became steadily more sophisticated so much so that by the time Samantha was four, she was able to proudly point out her name that she had written on her many pictures. A child's name is so important and being able to represent it with marks is a proud achievement and one that they take all opportunities to recreate! This is a good example of the meaning behind the marks. As John Matthews reminds, 'scribbles are products of a systematic investigation, rather than haphazard actions' (1999: 19). Samantha enjoyed talking about her pictures to her parents, 'I draw a horsey' she would announce as her interest in ponies showed. Her parents were so impressed by Samantha's achievement in writing that they spoke to her teacher and asked how they might extend her writing skills at home even further.

Reflection for early career professional

- What would your advice be to Samantha's parents in this case?

Reflection for leader/manager

- Would you agree that this is a great way to engage parents in children's learning. The challenge is how to sustain this same parental interest as Samantha gets older and her writing becomes more sophisticated. What practical messages might be given to Samantha's parents?

Parents can be involved in helping children to learn about number and shape through practical activities at home and practice and extend the mathematical skills and knowledge identified in the EYFS under Problem-Solving, Reasoning and Numeracy. When setting places for dinner a parent might ask the child, 'How many knives do we need so that everyone has one?' The potential for parents to exploit maths in variety of everyday situations is enormous – for example, matching, sorting, sand and water play, setting the table, in ways that link talk, play and learning. The old saying that 'Maths is everywhere' holds true when you begin to consider the opportunities in the home learning environment. Here are some examples. Equipment and materials are very evident in play that fosters mathematical understanding. For example: *Counting* – counting objects like plastic ducks, One, two, three . . . Counting aloud to a drum beat. Asking questions, 'How many cows can you see?'; Using photographs of the family to count the number of people.

Photograph 3.5 Parents Supporting Physical Development (© P. Hopkins)

Table setting; Counting snacks, Making objects from playdough to represent numbers 1–5. Adding games. Knocking down skittles with beanbags and counting the numbers remaining. *Shape and Space* – Doing jigsaws; Matching pictures; What's in the bag? Making hand and footprints in sand and trying to put one's foot or hand back in exactly the same place. Pattern making using beads and cotton reels and peg boards. Constructing simple 2D shapes from pipe-cleaners. Shape-sorting toys. Construction toys like Brio and Lego, Mobilo. Repeating patterns with wrapping paper. Printing blocks. *Measuring* – throwing a beanbag and counting how far a jump with 1 or 2 feet is. Comparing sizes of small objects. Acting out stories like *The Three Bears*. Stacking beakers. Filling cups of different sizes and asking, 'How many cups will I need to fill the tea-pot?' Weighing and measuring out ingredients for cooking. Recording a child's height. Keeping a diary over a week. Telling the time and talking through the seasons using a calendar.

Transition to Key Stage 1 (5 to 7 years of age)

From 5 to 7 years, children consolidate the advances in physical growth and psychomotor capacity in the early childhood years. This period sees gains in height and weight and changes to body proportions. With these, come increases in physical abilities and qualitative and quantitative changes to their movement patterns. Fundamental movement skills that involve equipment, in locomotion (e.g. climbing, skipping, etc.); manipulative skills (e.g. handling, kicking, striking, catching and throwing) and in stability (e.g. balancing, swinging, rolling, etc.) become better coordinated and skill levels improve considerably.

The ability to use equipment with skill is also significant for children with motor difficulties. The condition known as developmental dyspraxia affects between 5 per cent and 18 per cent of people in the United Kingdom. In relation to school age children, this means that at least one child in every class is likely to be affected by such a condition (Dixon and Addy, 2004) and more boys than girls are affected by it. Difficulties are experienced in planning and organizing movement and while problems may have been identified earlier than five, the environments and routines in schools can expose its difficulties much more. These difficulties show themselves in many aspects of children's play and daily living where movement planning and coordination are required. One obvious area where these difficulties are readily seen is in tasks that involve equipment. Between 5 and 7 years, a child's difficulties in buttoning and unbuttoning a coat or remembering which peg to hang the coat on, using a knife and fork at lunch time become social skills problems. Avoidance strategies are common and many children avoid school lunches and the embarrassment they feel. Eating with fingers and choosing snack type foods can mask their inabilities to respond to social norms and expectations at such times. Getting changed for outdoor play becomes a major event when the child is unable to get the sequence of dressing right and takes an inordinate amount of time. In movement session, being the only child when the music stops to walk around the hall in a clockwise direction, instead of anti-clockwise suddenly is no longer funny. Other gross motor skills are equally problematic. Bouncing balls, throwing and catching, using large apparatus, skipping with ropes present major problems for dyspraxic children. Using paint brushes, cutting out with scissors, doing jigsaws and manipulating the computer mouse become frustrating activities to avoid and who wants to build a group model with someone who cannot use a glue stick properly? For these children the condition affects their feeling of self worth and self image. Let us look at the story of Amir.

Case study

Amir is a 4 year old boy who suffers from dyspraxia. From being a toddler, his parents noticed he had an awkward way of walking, as if it was a struggle for him. He was an active boy and engaged in a myriad of physical activities with his peers. As he entered Nursery, the difficulties he had with his gross skills became more obvious. He rarely used a trike or scooter when outdoors but loved to be in the centre of things. He would watch as Sarah, his Key Person would show him how to use a gardening fork and small trowel to plant bulbs in the garden area. Often he would try to do the same but found it difficult. Fastening the buttons on his coat to go outside was a real challenge. Inside he would talk knowledgeably about his paintings but his grip and posture at the easel were very unusual. When other children got together to make models or build with the bricks, Amir was keen to join in but because of the difficulties he had, was rarely asked to join a group. This made Amir quite sad.

Reflection for early career professional

- How could you ensure that Amir is included in activities like group model-making?

Reflection for leader/manager

- What advice would you give to Sarah, the Key Person?

In the EYFS, there is much freedom for children to express themselves creatively painting, drawing and making models. As they move into Key Stage 1 this is seen as an area in which children with the condition show lack of development. Drawings are disproportionate, lacking in control and accuracy. The dyspraxic child has difficulty in deciding which hand to use to draw and write with (Portwood, 1999) even though laterality is generally secure by 3 years. Handwriting presents many problems and the list by Dixon and Addy reveal the extent of these problems. Typically these are

- Poor pencil grip
- Abnormal posture
- Awkward position of the paper to the child
- Inaccurate hand-eye coordination
- Incorrect letter formation
- Incomplete letter formation
- Erratic sizing of letter forms
- Mixture of upper-and lower-case letters
- Poor alignment of writing on the page
- Lack of consistency in direction of ascenders and descenders
- Inconsistent spacing between words, either no spaces, too narrow or to wide
- Heavy or light pressure through the pencil. (Dixon and Addy, 2004: 67–8)

Practitioners should consider what practical strategies can be used to help all children access curriculum areas and be successful. Movement lessons can be made more inclusive by introducing nerf balls and waffle balls (these are those oddly shaped balls that behave in strange ways when thrown or kicked). Parachutes, balance boards and frisbees can be used creatively. Consider modifying the physical space by making playing areas shorter and removing barriers like nets, changing rules (e.g. no limits on the number of bounces allowed), adapting equipment such as balloons and soft balls instead of traditional balls. Reduce distractions like intense sunlight and noise. Allocate children a hoop to define their allocated space. Allow sufficient time to dressing before and after physical activity. Use picture cues to show what equipment to use or where it is stored. Use more music to help with rhythm. These are some ways to accommodate slower processing of information, facilitate motor planning and execution and make movement lessons more rewarding for dyspraxic children.

Play is still an important part of children's lives between the ages of 5 and 7. They continue to challenge themselves physically and test out their physical capabilities. Their risk assessment skills are improving although some children of this age are inclined to be impulsive and can over estimate their abilities. There are still times when they still need adult guidance but they should still be provided with opportunities to take some responsibility for their own safety. Learning about safety must take into account individual differences. One 6 year old may be able to cut a slice of bread safely with a sharp knife, whereas another may still require close supervision. Playgrounds are play spaces where principles of safety and risk management can be exemplified. Playgrounds that are exciting and stimulating, have areas for quiet play and spaces and equipment for active play can help improve social interaction and reduce aggression (Rivkin, 2000). Playground markings such as 2D shapes, ladders, dice, stepping stones and compass points allow games with simple equipment such as Hopscotch and Circle Dodge ball that engage children actively. Skipping games and challenges like, 'How many skips can you do in 30 seconds?' are always popular and are great endurance builders (see the British Heart Foundation *Jump Rope For Heart Programme* for further information). Catching games like Prison Wall, Dog and Bone or Farmer, Farmer, May We Cross Your Golden River? require a modicum of equipment to be fun and are extremely energetic! Less energetic games often involve parachutes which can involve large number so children and are excellent for social skills but also can link to language and maths.

To resource playgrounds appropriately requires planning and also investment. The commitment to build or upgrade playgrounds and set up new supervised adventure playgrounds was outlined in the Children's Plan (2007). The *Play Strategy* set out a vision to improve play opportunities in all communities, and to rebuild 3,500 playgrounds and make them accessible to disabled children. Pathfinder projects will see the Government invest £235m in play spaces and are already under way to affirm their commitment to creating play spaces that meet individual and community needs. Pip ca\rd 3.3 in the EYFS reminds us that indoor and outdoor spaces must be secure, and safe yet challenging. The Children's Plan states that: 'supervised and unsupervised outdoor activities are important for children's development and also to reduce obesity, build social and emotional resilience, develop social skills, strengthen friendships, help children learn how to deal with risks – and of course because children enjoy them' (DCSF, 2007: 28).

The outdoors offers wonderful opportunities to be creative with spaces and materials. Garden areas provide great opportunities for children to dig and use trowels and small forks. Nature trails are easily set up. Bird tables and feeder boxes, bird and bat boxes, butterfly gardens will enhance a garden area. Mazes, attractive fencing and container pots of flowers and hanging baskets add instant colour and life. Sandpits and covered play spaces are great for developing talk and manipulative skills. Having a tap outside will allow endless hours of filling buckets and in inclement weather there is the added delight of mud! (Mud is actually a great medium to paint with and is easily washed off surfaces afterwards). Dens can be built or tents erected to encourage some private space for reflection. Putting up a swing on a sturdy tree will promote confidence and encourage climbing skills. Initial audits of available space can help thinking about the types of equipment and resources and how they should be used. There should be a natural area for children to explore the natural world, reflect and hide in; a gardening area to grow vegetables and small plants; a separate area for wheeled toys often with sheds and parking bays and marked roadways; a place to play with small games equipment; an open space to run around in and a climbing area with fixed frames as well as equipment to use in obstacle courses like A-frames, planks, tunnels and tyres. Margaret Edgington stresses that resources do not have to be expensive and provides a useful list that include

- milk crates
- old sinks
- ropes
- wind chimes

- cardboard tubings
- brooms with handles cut short
- balls of different sizes
- wellington boots
- recycled boxes
- flower pots
- shells
- tyres
- logs
- planters
- garden tools
- camping equipment
- umbrellas
- picnic set
- buckets
- dressing up clothes
- hanging baskets
- plastic piping
- blankets, sheets
- steering wheels. (Source, Edgington, 2002: 15).

Resources that offer children a broader experience include mark-making resources – that is, trolleys on wheels equipped with paper, writing materials, chalks, crayons, etc.; construction that include plans of buildings, clipboards to sketch with, etc.; resources for imaginative play for children to act out personal narratives through, for example, ambulance, airport, farms, market stall, fast-food stall or garden centre. In addition, natural resources such as sand, water, bark, wood shavings, conkers and pebbles; resources to develop control of the body to balance on, push or pull, roll and to include obstacle courses; creative resources to bark rubbing, printing, making collages; resources for scientific investigation that includes kites, windmills, flags, mirrors and books of fiction and non-fiction type to listen to stories or refer to (Edgington, 2002). Using the above will provide practitioners with many opportunities to join with the children outdoors and to involve other agencies. On a recent visit to a Nursery, local forest rangers had been working with a group of childminders. The childminders read a story to the children under cover of an awning, they hunted for the animals in the story, went on a wonderful forest trail led by the rangers and everyone finished in the day in a giant circle with parachute games. Part of a weekly activity session that was different each time and involved, and was thoroughly enjoyed by children and adults.

Children's perceptions of progressing from the EYFS into Key Stage 1 still reflect the store they place on mastering physical skills. In Year 1 classroom we visited several weeks into the autumn term, the children had been asked to reflect on their journey into Year 1. The teacher had captured their writing and drawings on a display entitled, 'Our hopes and fears going into Year 1'. Min, a Chinese boy wrote:

'I can ron veri fast. I can play with lego. I can play on a PS and tois. I can play bal. I can dress myself'.

As you can see, his understanding of how his learning journey is continuing shows a number of skills he has now achieved. Notice also, how significant equipment like toys are in this journey. Differences in the approach between EYFS and National Curriculum raise concerns for some educators who see the key stages as imposing unnecessary barriers for children and give confusing messages to teachers. With growing recognition that the principles of EYFS have much to offer later years of schooling and that approaches to teaching and learning here are relevant to Key Stage 1 and 2, with many teachers welcoming such an interface (Doherty and Brennan, 2008). Difficulties for children, teachers and parents in the transition from the then Foundation Stage to National Curriculum were reported in the influential EPPE study (Sylva, K. et al., 2003). Key findings of this study were that children valued their experiences in Reception and regretted the loss of opportunities to learn through play. Coming into Year 1, some found writing difficult and were bored by the requirement to sit and listen for long periods. On the other hand, many enjoyed the status of being more grown up and welcomed the learning challenges presented in Year 1. Teachers felt the biggest challenge was the move from a play-based approach in the Foundation Stage to a more 'structured' curriculum in Key Stage 1. Parents wanted to know what would be expected of their children, so they could help them prepare for Year 1 (EPPE, 2003, iii).

One of the few writers who has identified this division between the two age phases in physical development and physical education is Lavin (2003). His findings, presented in Table 3.3 highlight differences in teaching and learning approaches between them.

Certainly there are differences identified here but there are also a number of overlaps between the age phases. With regard to a physical development and physical education interface, there is growing recognition (Doherty and Brennan, 2008) that the principles of EYFS have much to offer the later years

Table 3.3 Differences in teaching and learning in Physical development in Foundation Stage and PE at Key Stage 1

Foundation Stage Physical Development	Key Stage 1 National Curriculum
Play-centred Exploration Experimentation	Skill focus Teacher directed Subject-based
Range of equipment Creativity Autonomy	Developing & selecting, applying skills Limited equipment Co-operative working
Manipulation Co-ordination Confidence	Exercise and health notions Composition Evaluate and improve performance
Increasing control Understanding Responses to rhythm, music, story	Watching & listening Expression of feelings through movement Remember and repeat skills and actions

of schooling and that approaches to teaching and learning here are relevant to Key Stage 1 and 2, with many teaches welcoming such an interface.

Reflection for early career professional

- How might Reception teachers support children's physical development at the transition point as they move into KS1? How can the balance be struck between the play focus in EYFS and more structured approach to NCPE in KS1?

Reflection for leader/manager

- Do you have a policy on transition? How does this make for a smooth transition from the EFYS into Key Stage 1 in practice? What are the key messages to be given out to ensure seamless transitions and a continuation of a child's learning journey?

References

Anning, A. (1991) *The First Years at School.* Milton Keynes: Open University Press

Anning, A. and Edwards, A. (1999) *Promoting Children's Learning for Birth to Five.* Buckingham: Open University Press

Alexander, G. M. and Hines, M. (2002). 'Sex differences in response to children's toys in nonhuman primates (Cercopithecus aethiops sabaeus)'. *Evolution & Human Behavior* 23, 467–79

Alexander, G. M. (2003). 'An evolutionary perspective of sex-typed *toy* preferences: Pink, blue, and the brain'. *Archives of Sexual Behavior* 32, 7–14

Almqvist, B. (1994) 'Educational toys, creative toys', in J. H. Goldstein (ed), *Toys, Play and Child Development*. New York: Cambridge University Press, pp. 46–66

Avery, J. G and Jackson, R. H. (1993) *Children and their Accidents*. London: Edward Arnold

Beunderman, J., Hannon, C. and Bradwell, P. (2007) *Seen and Heard: Reclaiming the public realm with children and young children*. London: Demos

Bloom, B. (1964) *Stability and Characteristics in Human Change*. New York: Wiley

Brady, L. -M., Gibb, J., Henshall, A. and Lewis, J. (2008) *Play and Exercise in Early Years: Physically active play in early childhood provision*. London: DCSF/NCB

Bruce, T. (1991) *Time to Play in early Childhood Education*. London: Hodder & Stoughton.

Casey, T. (2005) *Inclusive Play: Practical Strategies for Working with Children aged 3 to 8*. London: Paul Chapman

Community Playthings. (2005) *Creating Places for Birth to Threes – Room Layout and Equipment*. East Sussex: Community Playthings

Connolly, J., Doyle, A. B. and Reznick. E. (1988) 'Social pretend play and social interaction in preschoolers'. *Journal of Applied Developmental Psychology* 9, 301–13

Creasey, G. L., Jarvis, P. A. and Berk, L. E. (1998) 'Play and social competence', in O. N. Saracho and B. Spodek (eds), *Multiple perspective son Play in Early Childhood Education*. Albany: SUNY Press, pp. 116–43

David, T., Goouch, K., Powell, S. and Abbott, L. (2003) *Birth to Three Matters: A Review of the Literature*. Nottingham: DfES Publications

DCMS. (2004) *Getting Serious About Play – A review of children's play*. London: Department for Culture Media and Sport

DCSF. (2007) *The Children's Plan*. London: DCSF

DCSF. (2008a) *Practice Guidance for the Early Years Foundation Stage .Statutory Framework for the Early Years Foundation Stage: Setting the Standards for Learning, Development and Care for Children from Birth to Five*. London: DCSF

DCSF. (2008b) *It's Child Play. Early Years Foundation Stage*. Nottingham: DCSF

DCSF. (2008c) *Fair Play – A consultation on the play strategy*. London: DCSF

DfES. (2002) *Birth to Three Matters: A Framework to Support Children in their Earliest Years*. London: DfES

Dixon, G. and Addy, L. (2004) *Making Inclusion work for children with dyspraxia. Practical strategies for teachers*. London: Routledge Falmer

Doherty, J. and Bailey, R. (2003) *Supporting Physical Development and Physical Education in the Early Years*. Buckingham: Open University Press

Doherty, J. and Brennan, P (2008) *Physical education and development 3–11*. Abingdon, Oxon: David Fulton/Routledge

Doherty, J., Brock, A., Brock, J. and Jarvis, P. (2009) 'Born to Play: Babies and Toddlers Playing', in A. Brock, S. Dodds, P. Jarvis. and Olusoga, Y (eds), *Perspectives on Play. Learning for Life*. London: Pearson Education Limited, p. 98

DSCF. (2007) *The Children's Plan. Building Brighter Futures.* The Stationary Office: London

Dunn, J. (2004) *Children's Friendships: The Beginning of Intimacy.* Oxford: Blackwell

Early Childhood Forum (ECF). (2008) *It's all about play . . .* London: National Children's Bureau

Edgington, M. (2001) 'Mind and Body'. *Nursery World.* 16–22

Edgington, M. (2002) *The Great Outdoors. Developing Children' S Learning Through Outdoor Provision.* London: The British Association for Early Childhood Education

Elardo, R., Bradley, R. and Caldwell, B. M. (1975). 'The relation of infants' home environments to mental test performance from 6 to 36 months: A longitudinal analysis'. *Child Development* 46, 71–6

Froebel, F. (1906) *The Education Of Men.* New York: Appleton

Garvey, C. (1990) *Play.* Cambridge, MA: Harvard University Press

Glassy, D. and Romano, J. (2003). 'Selecting appropriate toys for young children: The pediatrician's role'. *American Academy of Pediatrics* 111, 911–13

Goldschmied, E. (1987) *Infants at Work* (training video). London: National Children's Bureau

Goldschmied, E. & Jackson, S. (1994) *People Under Three: Young Children in Day Care.* London: Routledge

Goldschmied, E. and Jackson, S. (2004) *People under Three, Young Children in Day Care,* 2nd edn. London: Routledge

Good Toy Guide. (2009) *http://www.natll.org.uk/index.php?page_id=37)*

Goswami, U. (2004) 'Neuroscience and education'. *British Journal of Educational Psychology* 74, 1–14.

Guddemi, M., Jambor, T. and Skrupskelis, A. (eds), (1999) *Play in a Changing Society.* Little Rock, AR: SECA

Gurian, M. (2001) *Boys and Girls learn Differently. A Guide for Teachers and Parents.* San Francisco: Jossey-Bass

Gura, P. (1992) *Exploring Learning: Young Children and Blockplay.* London: Paul Chapman

Gussin-Paley, V. (1984) *Boys and Girls: Superheroes in the Doll Corner.* Chicago: University of Chicago Press

Hodgson, J. (2001) *Mastering Movement.* London: Methuen

Hughes, A. M. (2006) *Developing Play for the under 3s: The Treasure Basket and Heuristic Play.* London: David Fulton

Hughes, F. (1999). *Children, Play, and Development,* 3rd edn. Boston: Allyn and Bacon.

Hutt, S. J., Tyler, C. and Christopherson, H. (1989) *Play, Exploration and Learning.* London: Routledge

Isenberg, J. P. and Jalongo, M. R. (2000). *Creative expression and play in early childhood,* 3rd edn. Upper Saddle River, NJ: Merrill/Prentice Hall

Lasenby, M. (1990) *The Early Years. A Curriculum for Young Children. Outdoor Play.* London: Harcourt Brace Jovanovich

Lavin, J. (2003) 'Physical development into physical education: is it fair play?' in H. Cooper and C. Sixsmith (eds), *Teaching Across the Early Years 3–7.* London: Routledge

Marin, C. (ed.), (2004) *Writing in the Air*. Maidstone: Kent County Council.

Matthews, J. (1999) *The Art of Childhood and Adolescence: The Construction of Meaning*. London: Falmer

Matterson, E. (1965) *Play with a Purpose for Under-Sevens*. London: Penguin

Maude, P. (2001) *Physical Children, Active Teaching*. Buckingham: Open University Press

Murata, N. and Maeda, J. (2002). 'Structured play for preschoolers with developmental delays'. *Early Childhood Education Journal* 29, 4, 237–40

National Playing Fields Association/Children's Play Council/PLAYLINK (2000) *Best Play: What play provision should do for children*. London: NPFA

Newcomb, A. F. and Bagwell, C. L. (1995) 'Children's friendship relations: A meta-analytic review'. *Psychological Bulletin* 117, 306–47

National Institute for Health and Clinical Excellence (NICE). (2009) *Promoting Physical Activity, Active Play and Sport for Pre-School and School-Age Children and Young People in Family, Pre-School, School and Community Settings*. London: NICE

O'Brien, M., Jones, D., Sloan, D. and Rustin, M. (2000) 'Children's independent spatial mobility in the urban public realm'. *Childhood* 7, 3, 257–77

Ouvry, M. (2003) *Exercising muscles and minds. Outdoor play and the early years curriculum*. London: National Children's Bureau

Palmer, S. (2006) *Toxic Childhood. How the Modern World is Damaging our Children and What We Can Do About It*. London: Orion

Pellegrini, A. D., Horvat, M. and Huberty, P. (1998). 'The costs of physical play in children'. *Animal Behaviour* 55, 1053–61

Portwood, M. (1999) *Developmental Dyspraxia. Identification and intervention. A Manual for Parents and Professionals* 2nd edn. London: David Fulton Publishers

Power, T. G. (2000). *Play and Exploration in Children and Animals*. London: Lawrence Erlbaum Associates

Pulaski, M. A. (1973) 'Toys and imaginative play', in J. L. Singer (ed.), *The Child's World of Make-Believe*. New York: Academic Press

Rivkin, M. (2000) *Outdoor experiences for young children*. *ERIC Clearinghouse on Rural Education and Small Schools*. Charleston WV: ERIC Digest

Rosen, B. and Peterson, L. (1990). 'Gender differences in children's outdoor play injuries: A review and integration'. *Clinical Psychology Review* 10, 275–94

Sammons, P., Elliot, K., Sylva, K., Melhuish, E., Siraj-Blatchford, I. and Taggart, B. (2004) 'The impact of pre-school on young children's cognitive attainments at entry to reception'. *British Educational Research Journal* 30, 5, 691–712

Sayeed, Z. and Guerin, E. (2000) *Early Years Play. A Happy Medium for Assessment and Intervention*. London: David Fulton Publishers

Shackell. A., Butler, N and Ball, D. (2008) *Design for Play: A Guide to Creating Successful Play Spaces*. Nottingham: Play England/ DCSF

Singer, J. L. (1994) 'Imaginative play and adaptive development', in J. H. Goldstein (ed), *Toys, Play and Child Development*. Cambridge: Cambridge University Press, p. 19

Sylva, K., Melhuish, E., Sammons, P., Siraj-Blatchford, I., Taggert, B. & Elliot, K. (2003). *The Effective Provision of Pre-School Education (EPPE) Project: Findings from the Pre-School Period.* London: Institute of Education

Vygotsky, L. S. (1978) *Mind and Society.* Cambridge, MA: Harvard University press.

Werner, P. and Burton, E. (1979) *Learning through Movement.* New York: Mosley.

Wood, L. and Bennett, N. (1997) The rhetoric and reality of play: teachers' thinking and classroom practice. *Early Years: The Professional Association of Early Years Education.* 2, 22–32

Conclusion

The series editors and authors hope that you find this book of interest and use to you in your professional work. If you would like to read more about the subject area, we recommend the following reading and websites to you.

Further reading

Brady, L-M., Gibb, J, Henshall, A. and Lewis, J. (2008) *Play and Exercise in Early Years: Physically Active Play in Early Childhood Provision.* London: DCSF/NCB

British Heart Foundation. *Jump Rope For Heart Programme.* London: BHF

Child Accident Prevention Trust. (2009) *Safety in Day Care and Play Settings. A Guide to Child Accident Prevention for Childminders and Organisers of Other Care And play Facilities.* London: CAPT

Community Playthings. (2008) *Creating Places for Birth to Threes.* East Sussex: Community Playthings

Doherty, J. Brock, A., Brock, J. and Jarvis, P. (2009) 'Born to Play: Babies and Toddlers Playing', in A. Brock, S. Dodds, P. Jarvis. and Olusoga, (eds), *Perspectives on Play. Learning for Life.* London: Pearson Education Limited

Doherty, J. and Bailey, R. (2003) *Supporting Physical Development and Physical Education in the Early Years.* Buckingham: Open University Press

Garrick, R. (2004) *Playing Outdoors in the Early Years.* London: Continuum

Health Education Authority. (1992) *Happy Heart's Playground Pack – HEA Happy Heart Project.* Surrey: Thomas Nelson and Sons Ltd

Hill, S. (1997) *Active Fun with Playground Markings.* Hull: Research Unit for PE, Sport and Health, University of Hull

Johnston, J and Nahmad-Williams, L. (2009) *Early Childhood Studies.* Harlow: Pearson Education

Maude, P. (2001) *Physical Children, Active Teaching: Investigating Physical Literacy.* Buckingham: Open University Press

National Institute for Health and Clinical Excellence (2009) *Promoting Physical Activity, Active Play and Sport for Pre-School and School-Age Children and Young People in Family, Pre-School, School and Community Settings.* London: NICE

Ouvry, M. (2003) *Exercising muscles and minds. Outdoor play and the early years curriculum.* London: National Children's Bureau

Pickup, I. and Price, L. (2007) *Teaching Physical Education in the Primary School.* London: Continuum

Useful websites

Birth to Three Matters: A Review of the Literature. This is the literature review which informed the formulation of the Birth-Three Matters document. This document has now been subsumed by the curriculum requirements for the Early Years Foundation Stage (DCFS, 2008) but it contains some very worthwhile information on physical development.

Both good sites on safety issues and providing sound guidance.

Good site for information on toys and the benefits and skills they promote

http://www.dfes.gov.uk/schoollunches/default.shtml

http://www.natll.org.uk/index.php?page_id=37).

http://www.standards.dcsf.gov.uk/eyfs/resources/downloads/rr444.pdf

Many useful articles on child nutrition.

The INPP website (The Institute for Neuro – Physiological Psychology). Look particularly at the section on the development of early childhood reflexes by Sally Goddard Blyth. *http://www.inpp.org.uk/reflexes/index.php*

The teachernet website on physical education and school sport. This site is also a gateway to many current publications in this area of learning. *http://www.teachernet.gov.uk/teachingandlearning/subjects/pe/*

This gives information about the compulsory nutritional standards for school lunches.

This is the website for the National Healthy Schools Programme.

This supports the work of Healthy Schools in all aspects of food in schools.

www.foodinschools.org.uk

www.rospa.org.uk

www.safehome.org.uk

www.schoolfoodtrust.org.uk.

www.wiredforhealth.gov.uk

If you would like to read more about other key areas of the Early Years Foundation Stage, please see the following:

Communication, Language and Literacy, by Callander, N and Nahmad-Williams, N. (London: Continuum, 2010)

Creative Development, by Compton, A., Johnston, J., Nahmad-Williams, L and Taylor, K. (London: Continuum, 2010)

Knowledge and Understanding of the World, by Cooper, L., Johnston, J., Rotchell, E. and Woolley, R.. (London: Continuum, 2010)

Personal, Social and Emotional Development, by Broadhead, P., Johnston, J., Tobbell, C. and Woolley, R. (London: Continuum, 2010)

Problem Solving, Reasoning and Numeracy, by Beckley, P., Compton, A., Johnston, J. and Marland, H. (London: Continuum, 2010)

Index